der

BOOK

Art of Disneyland

Disney Insider

YEARBOOK

2005

YEAR IN REVIEW

EDITIONS

NEW YORK

For information address Disney Editions, 114 Fifth Avenue, New York, New York 10011-5690.

Disney Editions

    Editorial Director: Wendy Lefkon
    Senior Editor: Jody Revenson
    Editorial Assistant: Jessica Ward
    Project Consultant: Jeff Kurtti
    Designer: Bruce Gordon
    Photo Editors: Jim Fanning, Ed Squair

    The book's producers would like to extend special thanks to Christine Cadena, Andrew Flatt, Jonathan Garson, Howard E. Green, Joel Hile, Michael J. Jusko, Debbie Morgan, Mary Mullen, David Roark, Thomas Schumacher, Diane Scoglio, and Robert Tieman.

Disney Online Group

    Ken Goldstein: Executive Vice President & Managing Director Disney Online
    Robert Gonsalves: Vice President, Production/Operations
    Joanne Erickson: Director, Marketing
    Kayvan Sotoodeh: Senior Art Director
    Cathy Georges: Senior Writer

    The Disney Online Group would like to extend special thanks to Ramon Alanes, Shari Arison, Mark Brogger, Jason Gino, Kim Grauer, Brett Hardin, Marleine Pacilio, and Malinda Talbot.

Library of Congress Cataloging-in-Publication Data on file.
ISBN: 1-4231-0151-0 (tr. ed.)
ISBN 1-4231-0152-9 (pbk.)

Printed in the United States of America
First Edition
10 9 8 7 6 5 4 3 2 1

Table of Contents

Disney in Depth

From the Vault

Fond Farewells

INTRODUCTION

Welcome to the first-ever *Disney Insider Yearbook*, the newest way to share in the Disney legacy. We hope this annual book will be a great way for true Disney fans to look back on the magic of the past year and to gaze ahead toward the magic yet to come.

This inaugural volume is packed with highlights from a highlight-filled year, including: our global Happiest Celebration on Earth, honoring Disneyland's 50th anniversary; the opening of the fantastic new Hong Kong Disneyland; a look at box-office hits such as *Chicken Little* and *The Chronicles of Narnia: The Lion, the Witch and the Wardrobe*; and a tribute to the exceptional individuals who were inducted as Disney Legends.

The Disney Insider Yearbook will also focus on the years ahead. That's fitting, because so much of our time is spent planning and creating new experiences for you to enjoy in the future. In this year's edition, you'll see the hard work that is currently underway for events that will be unveiled in 2006—such as the creation of the "Tarzan" stage musical, the exciting new motion pictures *Pirates of the Caribbean: Dead Man's Chest* and Disney/Pixar's *Cars*, as well as the opening of our newest attraction at Disney's Animal Kingdom Park, Expedition Everest.

More than seventy-five years ago our company founder, Walt Disney, began our journey with the vision we still hold today: to pioneer family entertainment that brings us closer together. We hope this collector's item helps you recall your own special memories of 2005, as it has for all of us who share this dream we call Disney.

Your friends at the Disney Insider Yearbook

Look for this special icon throughout the book!

Go to

Insider

www.Disney.com/DisneyInsider

Whenever you see it, please visit Disney Insider online at
www.Disney.com/DisneyInsider
to find more Insider information and related subjects

In addition to producing myriad Disney memories for our guests, 2005 marked a significant milestone in our corporate history. On October 2, 2005, Robert A. Iger assumed the role of chief executive officer of The Walt Disney Company, succeeding Michael D. Eisner, who retired after leading Disney for twenty-one years.

"It is truly an honor to be entrusted with the responsibility of guiding this great company that occupies such an important place in the hearts and minds of millions the world over, toward a very bright future," Bob said. "It's also an honor to work with our incredibly talented and dedicated worldwide team. I feel all the more privileged to succeed Michael, whose enormous accomplishments and tremendous leadership over more than two decades have built this company into the world's preeminent leader in family entertainment."

ABOVE: Michael Eisner *(left)* welcomes Bob Iger to his new role.

As Disney's president and chief operating officer, Bob worked with Michael in overseeing all aspects of The Walt Disney Company's operations on a worldwide basis. The heads of all of Disney's business units reported to both Michael and Bob. Bob first became part of Disney's management team in 1996, when The Walt Disney Company acquired Capital Cities/ABC, where he had been president and chief operating officer.

When Michael took the helm at Disney on September 22, 1984, the company had a modest value of $3 billion and had just survived battles with corporate raiders who wanted to take it over, break it up, and sell off its parts. Michael and then-president Frank Wells quickly rallied the Disney team, embarking on a journey that would awaken a sleeping giant and turn it into one of the world's largest—and most beloved—entertainment companies. On September 30, 2005, his last day at Disney, Michael was leaving a company valued at $60 billion.

"It is with a considerable amount of satisfaction and even pride that I approach the end of my term as CEO of this company," Michael said, following the Disney board's announcement of Bob as his successor. "There is a tinge of sadness added to these emotions, similar to the feeling one experiences at the end of a great day at Disneyland as one pulls into the station after the final E-ticket ride."

Eisner added, "I thank members of our management team, our entire cast, our shareholders, and the men and women who serve or have served on our board, for their enthusiasm and support for The Walt Disney Company. And mostly I thank Walt Disney—for bringing to us a culture and a mouse."

RED CARPET

CINDERELLA WEST COAST PREMIERE

Hollywood, California, September 15, 2005

A red-carpet event at the El Capitan theater on Hollywood Boulevard celebrated the Platinum Edition DVD release of *Cinderella*. Among the panelists on hand to discuss the film were Ilene Woods-Shaughnessy (Cinderella), Lucille Bliss (stepsister Anastasia), June Foray (Lucifer the cat), veteran Disney animator Andreas Deja, and one of the original "Nine Old Men" of Disney Animation, Ollie Johnston.

SKY HIGH PREMIERE

Hollywood, California, July 24, 2005

A superstar cast attended the premiere of the superhero comedy. During the after-party at Disney's Soda Fountain and Studio Store, stars Lynda Carter and Kelly Preston engaged in some High jinks.

THE GREATEST GAME EVER PLAYED PREMIERE

*Hollywood, California,
September 25, 2005*

Walt Disney Studios' new golfing drama teed off at the El Capitan theater with help from young stars Josh Flitter and Shia LaBeouf.

LILO & STITCH 2 PREMIERE

Oahu, Hawaii, August 15, 2005

Lilo and Stitch were among the many stars making a splash on Oahu's lush north shore for the launch of their new DVD, *Lilo & Stitch 2: Stitch Has a Glitch*.

DISNEY LEGENDS CEREMONY

Anaheim, California, September 20, 2005

Having just been honored as Legends at the 2005 Disney Legends Awards, Art Linkletter and Steve Martin leave their handprints for posterity. Linkletter was one of three hosts for Disneyland's grand opening telecast in 1955, while Martin honed his talents as a cast member in Merlin's Magic Shop in Fantasyland.

FESTIVAL OF THE LION KING PREMIERE PERFORMANCE

Hong Kong, China, September 11, 2005

Bob Iger, president, COO, and then CEO-elect of The Walt Disney Company, dedicated the premiere performance of "Festival of the Lion King." Performed in Hong Kong Disneyland's Theater in the Wild, the circus-style musical features dancing and music from Disney's animated classic *The Lion King*.

50TH ANNIVERSARY OF THE MICKEY MOUSE CLUB

Anaheim, California, October 3, 2005

Celebrating three significant milestones—the 50th anniversaries of Disneyland, *The Mickey Mouse Club*, and the Mouseketeers—the Disneyland Resort honored ten of the original Mouseketeers with the world's largest pair of "Mouseketeer Ears."

The display, held in the forecourt of Sleeping Beauty Castle, was made up of nearly a thousand people. Seen from above, the iconic black ears with the *Mickey Mouse Club* logo magically came alive and transformed to shimmering gold to mark the milestone occasion.

HONG KONG DISNEYLAND GRAND OPENING

Hong Kong, China, September 12, 2005

A traditional "lion dance" ritual in front of Sleeping Beauty Castle served as the centerpiece of Hong Kong Disneyland's grand-opening ceremonies. As part of the ritual, Zeng Qinghong, vice president of the People's Republic of China, and Michael Eisner, chief executive officer of The Walt Disney Company, "bring the lions to life" by painting their eyes on with red ink.

CHICKEN LITTLE PREMIERE

Hollywood, California, October 30, 2005

Stars Abby Mallard, Zach Braff, and Chicken Little rule the roost during the red-carpet premiere of Walt Disney Pictures' latest animated feature.

THE CHRONICLES OF NARNIA: THE LION, THE WITCH AND THE WARDROBE PREMIERE

London, England, December 7, 2005

The Royal Albert Hall hosted the world premiere and Royal film performance of Walt Disney Studios' and Walden Media's motion picture epic. Stars William Moseley, Skandar Keyes, Tilda Swinton, Georgie Henley, and Anna Popplewell were among the cast members in attendance. Nearby, Kensington Gardens was transformed into a winter wonderland for the after-party, which was attended by thousands of international guests.

HAPPIEST PLACES ON EARTH

THE HAPPIEST CELEBRATION ON EARTH

"The Happiest Celebration on Earth," an eighteen-month global commemoration of the 50th anniversary of the very first Disney theme park—Disneyland—continued throughout 2006, showcasing the largest debut of new Disney entertainment spectaculars and innovative adventures and attractions ever unveiled, such as: Walt Disney's Parade of Dreams, Disney's Block Party Bash, Remember. . . Dreams Come True fireworks, Disneyland: The First 50 Magical Years, Turtle Talk with Crush, Space Mountain, and Monsters, Inc., Mike & Sulley to the Rescue! (Disneyland Resort); Lights, Motors, Action! Extreme Stunt Show, "Cinderellabration," Lucky the Dinosaur, Soarin', and Expedition Everest (Walt Disney World Resort); Raging Spirits (Tokyo Disneyland Resort); Wishes fireworks (Disneyland Paris Resort); and the September 12, 2005, grand opening of Hong Kong Disneyland, Disney's eleventh vacation destination and first-ever theme park in China.

DISNEYLAND GOES TO THE HOLLYWOOD BOWL

Disneyland and Disney parks worldwide were the subject of three spectacular concerts (July 2–4, 2005) under the stars at the world-famous Hollywood Bowl. Before a combined audience of 54,000, John Mauceri, principal conductor of the Hollywood Bowl Orchestra, led the audience on a musical journey through five decades of "The Happiest Music on Earth" including songs from Pirates of the Caribbean, The Haunted Mansion, "it's a small world," Indiana Jones™ Adventure, Great Moments with Mr. Lincoln, and Soarin' Over California. Guest performers included Academy Award–winning songwriter Richard M. Sherman and legendary actor Fess Parker.

DISNEYLAND BECOMES A HOLLYWOOD "STAR"

Disneyland was honored on the occasion of its 50th anniversary by the Hollywood Historic Trust on July 14. In recognition of its pioneering status as an entirely new genre of family entertainment, Disneyland received the coveted Award of Excellence during a ceremony on Hollywood Boulevard (next to the historic El Capitan Theatre). A brass plaque was unveiled and placed adjacent to the constellation of stars along the famous Hollywood Walk of Fame.

SPACE MOUNTAIN RE-LAUNCH

Space Mountain blasted off into a new era of thrills on July 15, 2005, in a ceremony attended by legendary U.S. astronaut commander Neil Armstrong, the first man to step foot on the moon. The high-speed interstellar adventure re-opened following two years of being re-Imagineered for the 21st century featuring a new generation of special effects, rocket vehicles, sound track, and a smoother, darker ride.

PREMIERE OF TURTLE TALK WITH CRUSH

A new wave of fun washed ashore at Disney's California Adventure on July 15, 2005, as swimming Olympic gold medalist Amanda Beard helped to open Turtle Talk with Crush. The attraction experience features Crush, the sea turtle from the Walt Disney Pictures presentation of a Pixar Animation Studios film, *Finding Nemo*, and represents Disney's newest breakthrough in bringing favorite characters to life. From his digital world under the sea, Crush chats, plays, jokes, and reacts to guests in a unique, personalized way brought to life via an innovative combination of digital projection and sophisticated, voice-activated computer animation. A similar version of the attraction opened November 16, 2004, in The Living Seas pavilion at Epcot at Walt Disney World Resort in Florida.

DISNEYLAND TURNS 50!

Exactly fifty years after its gates opened for the first time, Disneyland honored the occasion of its actual golden anniversary with a spectacular rededication ceremony on July 17 featuring California governor Arnold Schwarzenegger, Michael D. Eisner, then-CEO of The Walt Disney Company, and Robert Iger, president, COO, and CEO-elect, The Walt Disney Company. Broadcast legend Art Linkletter (who hosted the live opening-day telecast on July 17, 1955) and Walt Disney's daughter, Diane Disney Miller, also joined the festivities to pay homage to the world's first Disney park.

Close to 10,000 people waited overnight inside Disney's California Adventure the evening of July 16 to be among the first inside Disneyland on its special day. Upon entering "The Happiest Place on Earth," each guest received a commemorative program and special gold Mickey "Ears" (specially engraved with the date). Main Street, U.S.A., soon became a sea of gold Mickey ears as everyone sang a heartfelt rendition "Happy Birthday" to Disneyland as the nostalgic ceremony in front of Sleeping Beauty Castle came to a rousing finale.

Throughout the day Guests received complimentary birthday cake (an astounding 100,000 cupcakes were served by the time the Park closed at midnight) while gigantic Jumbo-Trons were positioned throughout the resort in order to provide all guests with views of the ceremony and nostalgic images throughout the day.

"GOLDEN EARS" NATIONAL SURVEY

On July 11, Disney celebrated fifty years of theme park magic by announcing the results of a national consumer survey conducted by independent research firm Directive Analytics which revealed what America loves most about Disneyland Resort in California and Walt Disney World Resort in Florida. The Golden Ears Survey polled more than 8,000 consumers from all 50 states to gauge opinions about entertainment, attractions, characters, events, and occupations featured at Disney's flagship parks.

Topping America's list of favorite Disney theme park attractions is Space Mountain (63 percent), followed closely by Pirates of the Caribbean (62 percent) and The Haunted Mansion (49 percent).

The unique profession of Walt Disney Imagineer ties with Disney Tour Guide as the most sought-after Disney theme park role, according to the survey. Next in line is Jungle Cruise Skipper (14 percent), followed by Monorail Pilot (13 percent).

7

HONG KONG DISNEYLAND RESORT GRAND OPENING

Chinese pageantry mixed with Disney showmanship as the Hong Kong Disneyland Resort celebrated its official grand opening on Monday, September 12, 2005. In a spectacular ceremony in front of Sleeping Beauty Castle, set against the lush green mountains of Lantau Island, children welcomed guests in English, Cantonese and Putonghua. A hundred-voice Hong Kong Children's Choir performed the anthem "It's a Small World (After All)" and "One" (specifically written for Hong Kong Disneyland Resort), while dazzling Chinese acrobats and dancers, along with Disney ambassadors representing all of the Disney parks worldwide, participated in the historical event.

A highlight of the ceremony was a traditional Lion Dance in which the Lions are "brought to life" when their eyes are dotted with brushes of red ink, a tradition continued by Michael D. Eisner, Robert A. Iger, Zeng Qinghong, Vice-President of the People's Republic of China; and Donald Tsang, Chief Executive of the Government of the Hong Kong Special Administrative Region (HKSAR Government). The final ribbon cutting was performed by Eisner, Iger, Zeng and Tsang, and observed by Mickey Mouse, Minnie Mouse, and singer and Hong Kong Disneyland spokesperson Jacky Cheung.

The official grand opening of Hong Kong Disneyland Resort was preceded by a VIP weekend preview featuring such celebrities as Eason Chan, Emil Chau, Jacky Cheung, Andy Hui, Brad Kane, Coco Lee, Paige O'Hara, Lea Salonga, and Joey Yung.

FINDING NEMO SUBMARINE VOYAGE

On Friday, July 15, 2005, Jay Rasulo, chairman of Walt Disney Parks and Resorts, announced plans for the next major attraction coming soon to Disneyland Park—Finding Nemo Submarine Voyage. The all-new adventure will transform the fondly remembered Submarine Voyage and lagoon into an entirely unique underwater experience inspired by the Walt Disney presentation of the Pixar Animation Studios film, *Finding Nemo*. The attraction will introduce state-of-the-art Disney storytelling and showmanship, allowing guests to visit Nemo's computer generated world in a way that has never been done before.

EPCOT INTERNATIONAL FOOD AND WINE FESTIVAL 10TH ANNIVERSARY

The Epcot International Food and Wine Festival at Walt Disney World Resort celebrated its 10th anniversary September 30 through November 13. Featuring the all-new Disney's 10K Race for the Taste (October 9), the annual event featured more than twenty marketplaces with ethnic cuisine samples, including new adventures showcasing Turkey, Singapore, Puerto Rico, and Chile, plus a Spanish wine and cooking school joining the lineup of learning and tasting opportunities.

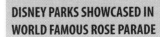

2005 NATIONAL THANKSGIVING TURKEY LANDS . . . AT DISNEYLAND!

The 2005 National Thanksgiving Turkey, named Marshmallow, was honored as the grand marshal of Disneyland's Thanksgiving Day parade on November 24. The famed turkey "gobbled" his way down Main Street, U.S.A., surrounded on a float by children dressed as Pilgrims and Native Americans. After the parade, the turkey retired to Santa's Reindeer Round-up in Frontierland to live happily ever after.

Following the traditional Presidential pardon of the National Thanksgiving Turkey in a White House ceremony on Tuesday, November 22, in Washington, D.C., the celebrated fowl became "The Happiest Turkey on Earth" and headed west to "The Happiest Place on Earth" —Disneyland! The National Thanksgiving Turkey flew first-class 2,288 miles nonstop to the West Coast for the special Thanksgiving Day honor.

DISNEY PARKS SHOWCASED IN WORLD FAMOUS ROSE PARADE

Walt Disney Parks and Resorts continued the fun and excitement of its global "Happiest Celebration on Earth" with a float entry entitled "The Most Magical Celebration on Earth" in the 2006 Pasadena Tournament of Roses. The float was highlighted by a floral depiction of the five Disney castles as seen in California, Florida, Japan, France, and Hong Kong. Soaring nearly 50 feet high and 150 feet long (the longest 2006 Rose Parade entry), the float featured the U.S. premiere of the newest Disney song "One," written exclusively for the recent grand opening of Hong Kong Disneyland. The float was comprised of over fifty distinct varieties of roses with plant material from each of the Disney theme park host countries and states. Sleeping Beauty Castle at Disneyland in Southern California stood prominent in the float design as the original Disney symbol of magic and happily-ever-afters.

EXPEDITION EVEREST OPENS AT DISNEY'S ANIMAL KINGDOM

In April, Expedition Everest opens at Disney's Animal Kingdom at Walt Disney World Resort in Florida, taking thrills to all-new heights in an unbelievable runaway train adventure. Featuring a terrifying encounter with the fearsome and mysterious Yeti that guards the route to Mount Everest, the attraction is one of the most complex ever created by Walt Disney Imagineering. Looming almost 200 feet high and occupying a footprint of 6.2 acres, the new iconic attraction features an authentic Himalayan village and an aging, industrial steam railway whose 34-passenger railcars take would-be explorers on a white-knuckle adventure into the icy unknown, braving twists, turns and sudden drops inside and outside the mighty mountain, leading to an unforgettable encounter. The trains of the Anandapur Rail Service take intrepid adventurers into a swirl of breathtaking spiral curves to a narrow escape from the powerful Yeti, the most mammoth and sophisticated Audio-Animatronics figure ever created by Disney's Imagineers.

EXPEDITION EVEREST: MISSION HIMALAYAS

From August through October 2005, Disney embarked on an extraordinary scientific and cultural journey to China and the eastern Himalayas to explore the legendary "realm of the Yeti." Conservation International and Discovery Networks joined Disney on *Expedition Everest: Mission Himalayas* in the search for new species and ancient legends.

Scientists from global conservation leader Conservation International and Disney's Animal Kingdom Park at Walt Disney World Resort in Florida searched for undiscovered species likely to live in these remote regions known as biodiversity hot spots, Earth's biologically richest and most threatened places. The team of internationally renowned biologists, botanists, and technical experts conducted a scientific inventory of plant and animal species in areas that are little known but potentially important conservation sites.

Imagineers joined the unique journey to investigate the powerful legend of the Yeti, bringing a new level of authenticity to Expedition Everest, the massive attraction at Disney's Animal Kingdom. Discovery Networks, renowned for compelling, real-world storytelling, tracked the expedition to share the unique adventure story with audiences throughout the globe.

NEW DISNEY CRUISE LINE ITINERARY

Passengers aboard the Disney *Magic* set sail for entirely new ports of call as the Disney Cruise Line introduces an all-new seven-night western Caribbean cruise itinerary which includes two visits to Disney's private island, Castaway Cay. This new itinerary debuts May 27, 2006.

On select dates the Disney *Magic* departs Port Canaveral on Saturday with a festive "Bon Voyage" send-off; the fun and sun of Castaway Cay is the highlight for Sunday; Monday provides a day on warm Caribbean seas; on Tuesday and Wednesday the *Magic* visits the ports of Costa Maya and Cozumel, respectively; Thursday is a day at sea; on Friday guests spend another fun-filled day on Castaway Cay; and on Saturday the *Magic* returns to its home port of Port Canaveral, Florida.

"MONSTERS" INVADE DISNEY'S CALIFORNIA ADVENTURE

The fun-filled new adventure Monsters, Inc., Mike & Sulley to the Rescue! opened in January 2006 during a star-studded "premiere" in the Hollywood Pictures Backlot of Disney's California Adventure Park at the Disneyland Resort. Inspired by the hit 2001 Disney/Pixar film *Monsters, Inc.* the elaborate new dark ride attraction stars the characters and residents of the child-adverse "Monstropolis." Featuring sixteen distinct show scenes, forty animated characters, the original voice talent from the film, and an interactive encounter with the irascible Roz, the all-new adventure leaves guests "screaming" with laughter!

DISNEYLAND PARIS INTROS BUZZ LIGHTYEAR LASER BLAST

Disney's trademark creative storytelling and state-of-the-art innovation combined to create Buzz Lightyear Laser Blast, an all-new interactive Disneyland Paris attraction that opened April 8, 2006. Inspired by a Walt Disney Pictures presentation of a Pixar Animation Studios film, *Toy Story 2*, guests aboard this new out-of-this-world adventure help Buzz Lightyear prevent the theft of the galaxy's energy supply by the evil Emperor Zurg. Would-be Space Rangers pilot their own 360-degree spinning, two-passenger Space Cruiser in order to hit targets with their own personal blaster cannon and gain points that will protect the peace of outer space.

AUTOPIA OPENS AT HONG KONG DISNEYLAND

In summer 2006, all roads at Hong Kong Disneyland led to the grand opening of Autopia—the first major attraction to be added to the Park since its opening. Like its predecessors, Autopia is located in Tomorrowland and features battery-powered vehicles with onboard lighting and audio effects. The Autopia highway at Hong Kong Disneyland is a three-lane thoroughfare winding through both formal gardens and surreal, "otherworldly" landscapes. Along their completely outdoor journey, drivers of tomorrow experience elevation changes that take them under and over bridges affording rich views of Tomorrowland. Guests aboard Autopia will discover a number of surprises as they navigate the winding highways and by-ways of Hong Kong Disneyland's newest attraction.

RAVEN TEAMS WITH MAKE-A-WISH TO BRIGHTEN CHILDREN'S LIVES

Four special little girls had their wish to meet Raven-Symoné granted during a surprise trip to New York City care of Disney and the Make-A-Wish Foundation.® The girls, ages seven to twelve, were flown in from Kentucky, Philadelphia, Illinois, and California with their families to be Raven's VIP guests for the launch party of the That's So Raven Mix Stick music player, fragrance, and cosmetics.

Alecia, Armani, Candi, and Samantha had their own private "green room," where stylists gave them a fun *That's So Raven* look with outfits from the clothing line based on the hit Disney Channel show. As they sat in their personalized *That's So Raven* director's chairs, makeup artists used the new Raven cosmetic line to add a little sparkle and shine to go with the twinkle already in the girls' eyes. Then it was on to the hairstylist, who fitted them with hair ornaments, hats, and a special new style for the big event.

After all the pampering, the four posed for photographers during a private shoot, and then it was time to meet Raven. The group discussed everything from their new clothes to their favorite *That's So Raven* episode to slumber parties. After the girl talk, it was off to the launch party, but not before each wish child was interviewed by Monica of Disney Channel 411.

At the end of the night, the girls went home with several *That's So Raven* outfits, goodie bags filled with everything Raven and, most important, many new friendships and memories!

Meeting Raven is the most popular television wish requested through the Make-A-Wish Foundation, and Raven is committed to the cause, having fulfilled fifty wishes since her show's inception. In total, Disney fulfills more than 5,000 wishes for Make-A-Wish each year. The majority of these experiences involve Disney's Parks and Resorts; however, they also include working with animators, meeting favorite characters, visiting the sets of Disney films or television shows and meeting Disney personalities.

To learn more about Disney's outreach programs, visit *www.disneyhand.com*.

THE MAKE-A-WISH FOUNDATION® AND DISNEY CELEBRATE 50,000TH DISNEY THEME PARK WISH

Christian Marlowe, a five-year-old from Coos Bay, Oregon, was all smiles today aboard a magic carpet when he, along with the Genie from *Aladdin*, a huge magic lamp, and a special cake, arrived in front of Sleeping Beauty Castle at Disneyland for a ceremony in his honor. Christian is the 50,000th child to have a Disney theme park wish granted by the Make-A-Wish Foundation and Disney. His special wish was simple: he wanted to visit Disneyland and meet Mickey Mouse.

In attendance with Christian, who has Duchenne muscular dystrophy, was his brother, Anthony, his sister, Jennifer, and his parents, Lisette and Alex. Also recognized during the ceremony was Octaviana Trujillo, who is the mother of Frank "Bopsy" Salazar—the very first child to have a wish granted by the Make-A-Wish Foundation and Disney twenty-five years ago. More than seventy-five other past and present wish children from around the U.S. and abroad also gathered as ambassadors for the week-long celebration, which also commemorates Make-A-Wish's twenty-fifth anniversary.

"Through all of our outreach programs, Disney is committed to granting wishes for children to brighten their lives, and the lives of their families, when they need it most," said Jody Dreyer, senior vice president, Disney Worldwide Outreach. "Each child in attendance here today serves as an inspiration to all children confronting life-threatening medical conditions," said Make-A-Wish Foundation President and Chief Executive Officer David Williams.

"Christian's wish is the beginning of something very special," said Lisette Marlowe. "If you have faith and believe that your child can become better, then they will. This is Christian's first time at Disneyland, and we are thrilled to see the joy on his face. When he is happy, we are too."

A Disney theme park visit remains the Foundation's most requested wish for children with life-threatening medical conditions. In fact, Disney fulfills more than 5,000 wishes for the Make-A-Wish Foundation each year through its corporate charitable outreach program.

The Make-A-Wish Foundation and Disney began their relationship in 1980, when Disney helped the newly formed charity grant its first wish to the then seven-year-old Salazar. He received three wishes as the first recipient: he wanted to go to Disneyland, he wanted to be a fireman, and he wanted to ride in a hot air balloon.

In addition to Disney's sponsorship of the 25th Anniversary Conference, American Airlines generously flew each ambassador and their family to California to mark the occasion.

DISNEY DONATES $2 MILLION TO MAKE-A-WISH FOUNDATION® ABOARD THE DISNEY *MAGIC*

Disney's once-in-a-lifetime, star-studded fund-raising event held aboard the Disney *Magic* cruise ship on the eve of the fiftieth anniversary of Disneyland generated more than $1 million for the Make-A-Wish Foundation.

After Michael Eisner presented the check to Make-A-Wish Foundation of America President and Chief Executive Officer David Williams, Bob Iger called upon Mickey Mouse and Minnie Mouse to present Williams with a surprise second check for $1 million dollars donated by the company.

The $2 million will benefit the Make-A-Wish Foundation of America and the Greater Los Angeles, Orange County, and Inland Empire, California, chapters, helping them continue their mission of granting the wishes of children with life-threatening medical conditions to enrich the human experience with hope, strength, and joy.

Those who attended the party and participated in the fun, interactive events with guests aboard the Disney Cruise Line ship included: Kelly Preston (*Sky High*), Paige Hemmis and Paul DiMeo (*Extreme Makeover: Home Edition*), Randy Jackson (*American Idol*), Raven-Symoné and Kyle Massey (*That's So Raven*), Amy Bruckner (*The Suite Life*), Christy Carlson Romano (*Kim Possible*), Kurtwood Smith (*That 70's Show*), Diane Disney Miller (Silverado Winery), Ashley Parker Snider (Fess Parker Winery & Vineyard), Mark Hoppus (Blink 182), Skateboarder Bob Burnquist, Los Angeles Dodgers Eric Gagne and Jason Phillips, Los Angeles Angel Tim Salmon, Los Angeles King Steve Avery, Green Bay Packer Ahman Green, and Cincinnati Bengal TJ Houshmanzadeh.

Honorary cruise directors, who helped to raise pre-awareness and support for the event, were: Jim Belushi, Candice Bergen, Tom Bergeron, Amanda Bynes, Jackie Chan, Johnny Depp, Jennifer Garner, Chris Harrison, Teri Hatcher, Tony Hawk, Felicity Huffman, Hugh Jackman, George Lopez, Garry Marshall, Christy Carlson Romano, John Stamos, and Raven-Symoné.

Disney's history of wish granting started when Walt Disney opened Disneyland in 1955 and hosted children from around the world. In 1980, Disney joined together with the newly launched Make-A-Wish Foundation to help grant the Foundation's first official wish — a trip to Dis-

neyland for seven-year-old Frank "Bopsy" Salazar. Today, Disney fulfills more than 5,000 wishes each year, with a Disney theme park visit remaining the Foundation's most-requested wish.

Other one-of-a-kind wish experiences requested include taking a Disney cruise, working with Disney animators, meeting favorite Disney talent and characters, or visiting the sets of Disney films and television shows.

Said Iger: "Walt Disney would be proud that on the eve of the fiftieth anniversary of Disneyland, we recognize, celebrate, and continue his legacy of making wishes come true through our work with the Make-A-Wish Foundation."

guests and signed autographs for fans. Since the debut of *That's So Raven* in 2003, Raven-Symoné has granted more than fifty wishes.

Said Williams: "This generous gift is just one example of the remarkable commitment Disney has made to the Make-A-Wish mission through the years. We thank them for underwriting this event so that all proceeds benefit the Make-A-Wish Foundation, and we look forward to continuing our special relationship with Disney in bringing hope, strength, and joy to children with life-threatening medical conditions."

Former wish recipients were also on hand to provide inspiration to the evening's special guests.

During the evening, one child had her special wish granted. The wish of twelve-year-old Elizabeth "Ashley" Gullap of Ripley, Mississippi, was to see what it's like to be a star and attend a red carpet event with Disney Channel's Raven-Symoné. Her dream was fulfilled when she arrived in a limousine and the two walked the red carpet together, posing for photographers and even participating in media interviews together. *American Idol*'s Randy Jackson joined the two on the carpet, surprising Ashley and greeting her with a big hug. Then it was on to Rockin' Bar D where the two greeted

Ohio's Travis Flores, fourteen and undergoing treatment for cystic fibrosis, had his book *The Spider Who Never Gave Up* published in 1999 and was on hand to sign autographs while celebrities read his story to children in attendance.

For more information about the Make-A-Wish Foundation, visit www.wish.org. For more information on Disney's philanthropic efforts, visit *www.disneyhand.com*.

SCREENING ROOM
FILM

VALIANT
August 19, 2005

From the producer of *Shrek* and *Shrek 2* came *Valiant*, the story of a small carrier pigeon who becomes a big World War II hero. Ewan McGregor (best known as Obi-Wan Kenobi in the three *Star Wars* prequels) voiced the titular character, and a host of well-known British talent (Ricky Gervais, Tim Curry, Jim Broadbent, John Cleese, and John Hurt) rounded out the supporting cast.

THE GREATEST GAME EVER PLAYED
September 30, 2005

It was a major sports upset: Francis Ouimet, a twenty-year-old amateur golfer with a caddie half that age, defied all expectations by beating reigning British champion Harry Vardon in the 1913 U.S. Open. Though it may sound like an unlikely story, this little-known incident served as the basis for *The Greatest Game Ever Played*, a sports drama cut from the same cloth as Disney's *The Rookie* and *Miracle*. Shia LaBeouf (*I, Robot* and *Holes*) stars as Ouimet, the working-class youth who defeats his idol Vardon (Stephen Dillane) and shakes up the genteel golf world. Actor Bill Paxton (*Mighty Joe Young*) directed the film, which screenwriter Mark Frost adapted from his nonfiction book of the same title.

GLORY ROAD
January 13, 2006

The themes of racial equality, sportsmanship, and personal dedication are central to *Glory Road*, the incredible true story of Texas Western basketball coach Don Haskins, who led college basketball's first all-black starting lineup to victory in the 1966 NCAA championship. Josh Lucas (*Sweet Home Alabama*) stars as Haskins, a Hall of Famer passionately dedicated to his team and his game. The film also features performances from Derek Luke (*Antwone Fisher*) and Jon Voight (*National Treasure*). Jerry Bruckheimer, who was responsible for the similarly inspiring sports film *Remember the Titans*, served as producer.

THE SHAGGY DOG
March 10, 2006

Tim Allen (*The Santa Clause*) stars in this remake of the classic 1959 Disney movie. The updated version tells the story of Dave Douglas (Allen), a lawyer who occasionally—and inconveniently—transforms into a large, shaggy sheepdog. While the unexpected changes from man to beast do little to help Dave's legal career, they do teach him about what it means to be a better family man.

EIGHT BELOW
February 17, 2006

How far would you go for a friend? If you're Arctic explorer Jerry Shepard, the answer is quite literally to the ends of the Earth. Paul Walker (*The Fast and the Furious*) plays Shepard, an explorer stationed at the United States research base in Antarctica. While on an expedition with his friend (Jason Biggs) and an American geologist (Bruce Greenwood), a terrifying accident forces Shepard to leave behind his team of eight sled dogs. Braving harsh terrain and extreme weather conditions, Shepard is determined to rescue the marooned animals, which are facing a months-long struggle for survival. It may sound like a fantastic story, but *Eight Below* was inspired by an actual Arctic expedition that took place in the late 1950s. The film was directed by Frank Marshall, who himself is no stranger to adventure and suspense, having co-produced the Indiana Jones trilogy and *The Sixth Sense*.

THIS YEAR'S SCREEN DEBUTS also included the barn-raising blockbuster *Chicken Little* (November 4, 2005; see page 84), and the epic fantasy *The Chronicles of Narnia: The Lion, the Witch and the Wardrobe*, which premiered December 9 to worldwide critical and public acclaim (see page 90). Coming to the big screen on July 7, 2006, is *Pirates of the Caribbean: Dead Man's Chest* (see page 102). The new Disney/Pixar comedy *Cars* speeds into cinemas on June 9, 2006 (see page 112). Read an in-depth article about each of these magnificent movies inside!

JOHNNY & THE SPRITES

Want to help your preschoolers get a sense of the world's magical possibilities? Then let them take a trip with Johnny T as he makes his way through Grotto's Grove, a magic forest where sprites, pixie dust, and talking animals and flowers are the norm.

Johnny & the Sprites is the brainchild of multitalented John Tartaglia, who serves as the show's creator, executive producer, and star. The Tony-nominated performer ("Avenue Q") was one of the youngest puppeteers ever to perform on *Sesame Street* (he was sixteen when he joined the cast). For his first major foray into series television he's culled some major talent that includes legendary Broadway composer Stephen Schwartz ("Godspell," "Wicked"), who contributes the program's theme song, and puppet designer Michael Schupach, whose work has been featured on Broadway in "Little Shop of Horrors" and "Avenue Q," as well as on Playhouse Disney's *Bear in the Big Blue House*. Currently an interstitial on Playhouse Disney, a full-fledged series of the same name is destined to hit the airwaves in 2006.

THE SUITE LIFE OF ZACK & CODY

The hit live-action series *The Suite Life of Zack & Cody* follows the escapades of twin twelve-year-old brothers Zack and Cody (played by real-life identical twins Dylan and Cole Sprouse) who inhabit a suite in the Boston hotel where their mother Carey (Kim Rhodes) is a headlining singer. The boys try their best to exploit the hotel's amenities—including the room service, the pool, the game room, and the candy counter—to full advantage. In the process, they befriend and run afoul of a lively assortment of characters that includes hotel manager Mr. Moseby (Phill Lewis), candy-counter clerk Maddie Fitzpatrick (Ashley Tisdale), and the spoiled daughter of the hotel's owner, London Tipton (Brenda Song).

DISNEY'S THE BUZZ ON MAGGIE

Set in the fly metropolis known as Stickyfeet, *Disney's The Buzz on Maggie* tracks the everyday life of Maggie Pesky, an unusually creative and expressive "tweenage" fly. Like all adolescents, Maggie is constantly struggling to find a balance between individuality and conformity. She's fun-loving, energetic, and always looking for a way to make her mark. Unfortunately, Maggie is also quite capable of ruffling the antennae of more conventional flies, and her actions inevitably disrupt the balance of the world around her—with unintended consequences.

MICKEY MOUSE CLUBHOUSE

Mickey, Minnie, Donald, Daisy, Goofy, and Pluto return to television in *Mickey Mouse Clubhouse*, a new computer-animated series on Playhouse Disney. Each episode encourages preschool viewers to participate as Mickey and his friends solve a series of easy-to-understand tasks and puzzles. The program represents Mickey's third series to be produced by Walt Disney Television Animation, following *Disney's House of Mouse* and *Mickey Mouseworks*.

LITTLE EINSTEINS

New to the Playhouse Disney lineup, Disney's *Little Einsteins* aims to entertain and engage the preschool set with a mix of globetrotting adventure, natural exploration, art, and classical music. Young viewers are encouraged to clap, sing, and dance along with Annie, Quincy, June, Leo, and their flying craft, Rocket, as they travel to famous locations around the world. The series, which was inspired by Disney's award-winning Baby Einstein line of infant developmental media, is notable for its unique blend of real-world locations with two-dimensional character animation.

TELEVISION

THE MUPPETS' WIZARD OF OZ

In May 2005, ABC's *The Wonderful World of Disney* brought the famed Muppets back to television in a new made-for-TV movie, *The Muppets' Wizard of Oz*. This contemporized spoof of L. Frank Baum's classic novel features Grammy Award–winning pop star Ashanti in the role of Dorothy, a Kansas teenager who dreams of escaping the rural life to become a big-time singer. Dorothy's reality is literally turned upside down when a tornado sweeps her and her pet prawn Toto to Oz, a magical land populated by—you guessed it—Muppets. Once in Oz, Dorothy encounters the Wizard (Jeffrey Tambor), who promises to turn her into a superstar—but only if she and new friends Scarecrow (Kermit), the Tin Thing (Gonzo), and the Cowardly Lion (Fozzie the Bear) can defeat the diabolical Wicked Witch of the West (played by the brilliantly cast Miss Piggy).

Stars Queen Latifah and David Alan Grier play Dorothy's aunt and uncle, and Oscar winner Quentin Tarantino has a terrifically funny cameo in which he coaches Kermit through a crucial confrontation. The movie also features original songs performed by Ashanti. In case you missed the ABC broadcast, *The Muppets' Wizard of Oz* is now available on DVD from Disney's Buena Vista Home Entertainment.

LITTLE HOUSE ON THE PRAIRIE

This past year, *The Wonderful World of Disney* brought Laura Ingalls Wilder's beloved 1935 novel *Little House on the Prairie* back to television. With a painstaking attention to even the smallest details of its literary source, this five-part, six-hour limited series tells the saga of the Ingalls, a turn-of-the-century pioneer family making its way across the Kansas Territory. In order to re-create the scope and majesty of the American Frontier, the series was shot on location over the course of four months in an unspoiled corner of Calgary, Alberta. The results of this location shooting are literally on the screen, as the program has a highly cinematic sense of place and of vista.

CELEBRATING DISNEYLAND'S 50TH, WONDERFUL WORLD-STYLE

In honor of Disneyland's 50th anniversary, ABC broadcast a series of specially produced "Happiest Celebration on Earth" celebrity interstitials during *The Wonderful World of Disney*. Airing over the seven weekends leading up to Disneyland's birthday, each segment was a star-studded event directly tied to some aspect of The Walt Disney Company's global commemoration. Among the highlights: John Goodman (*Monsters, Inc.*) hosted a spot featuring the new Block Party Bash at Disney's California Adventure and Buzz Lightyear Astro Blasters attraction at Disneyland; Lindsay Lohan (*Herbie: Fully Loaded*) was featured with a stunt car during a bit devoted to the new Lights, Motors, Action! Extreme Stunt Show at Disney Studios in Florida; and Ashanti (*The Muppets' Wizard of Oz*) held court during a segment about the new "Cinderellabration" at Walt Disney World. Capping off their run was an interstitial featuring Julie Andrews at Disneyland, plus a performance of the official theme song of Disneyland's 50th anniversary, "Remember When," by LeAnn Rimes. Airing on the evening of July 16, the segment served as a perfect lead-in for Disneyland's 50th birthday the very next morning.

CINDERELLA PLATINUM EDITION
Burbank, California, October 4, 2005

Cinderella, the most requested title in Disney's vault, has been made available on home video for the first time in nearly ten years. For its Platinum Edition DVD release, Disney digitally restored the film, gave it a 5.1 enhanced audio mix and included some spectacular bonus materials: two deleted scenes, making-of and behind-the-scenes featurettes, a storyboard-to-film comparison, and more.

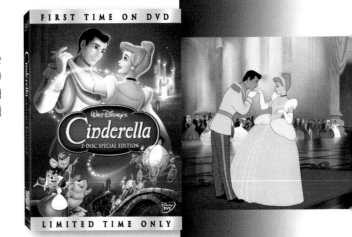

TOY STORY 10TH ANNIVERSARY EDITION AND
TOY STORY 2 SPECIAL EDITION
Burbank, California, September 6, 2005

Toy Story, the first full-length feature created entirely via computer animation, has been given the special treatment for its tenth anniversary home video release, allowing the adventures of Buzz and Woody to be enjoyed with enhanced picture and an all-new home-theater sound mix. The two-disc set includes deleted scenes, early animation tests, filmmaker commentary, and a retrospective with director John Lasseter. Looking for the perfect companion to the tenth anniversary release of *Toy Story*? Then check out the *Toy Story 2: Special Edition*, which also has enhanced picture and sound, as well as a raft of cool bonus features.

TARZAN SPECIAL EDITION
Burbank, California, October 18, 2005

Disney's animated adaptation of Edgar Rice Burroughs' *Tarzan* returns with a special-edition DVD filled with interactive games, a new Disneypedia featurette, deleted scenes (including an alternate opening), filmmaker's audio commentary, and other features.

HOME ENTERTAINMENT

HERBIE: FULLY LOADED
**Burbank, California,
October 25, 2005**

Herbie, star of four previous theatrical films, returns with new owner Maggie Peyton (Lindsay Lohan) behind the wheel. Together, the duo aims to break into the world of NASCAR and become its newest champs. The DVD release features exclusive bonus material such as deleted scenes, bloopers, and a behind-the-scenes look at NASCAR.

KRONK'S NEW GROOVE
Burbank, California, December 13, 2005

In this feature-length sequel to *The Emperor's New Groove*, muscle-bound henchman Kronk comes up with a get-rich-quick scheme that goes awry, helping him discover that real wealth comes from friendship and being "true to your groove." The film features the voice cast from the original *Groove*, including Patrick Warburton, David Spade, John Goodman, and Eartha Kitt, plus new cast members Tracey Ullman and John Mahoney. The movie has some great music from B5 and Earth, Wind and Fire, while the DVD itself is loaded with entertaining extras.

SKY HIGH
Burbank, California, November 29, 2005

At Sky High, the first and only high school for kids with superhuman powers, the student body is divided not into jocks and geeks but into heroes and sidekicks. For Will Stronghold (Michael Angarano), son of legendary superhero parents The Commander (Kurt Russell) and Jetstream (Kelly Preston), the bar is set especially high. But Will, who seemingly has no superpowers of his own, risks being relegated to the rank of sidekick—and no matter what, he'll still have to face the trials and tribulations of freshman year.

BAMBI II
Burbank, California, February 7, 2006

In this sequel to the Disney classic, Bambi's mother is gone, leaving his father, the Great Prince of the Forest (*Star Trek: The Next Generation*'s Patrick Stewart), little choice but to raise Bambi and teach him the ways of the forest. All of *Bambi*'s classic characters are on hand for the new film, while new ones are introduced (who knew Thumper had rambunctious sisters?).

IN GOOD COMPANY
PUBLISHING

A TOUCH OF PIXIE DUST

You didn't think Tinker Bell was the only fairy, did you? The possibility that she is but one of many pixies inhabiting Peter Pan's Never Land serves as the basis for Newbery Award–winning author Gail Carson Levine's brilliantly imagined new book, *Fairy Dust and the Quest for the Egg*. The story concerns Never Land newcomer Prilla, who has yet to find her fairy talent, and her quest to repair the broken egg of Mother Dove, who is the fount of Never Land's magic. Thanks to the enduring popularity of J.M. Barrie's *Peter Pan* novel and Disney's classic film, Tinker Bell will already be familiar to most readers. Levine, however, adds to the Never Land canon by introducing Tinker Bell's fairy friends, while also filling in the details of Tink's life in idyllic Fairy Haven. (Who knew, for example, that she'd still be miffed at Peter Pan over that "Wendy Incident"?) The resulting narrative has all the hallmarks of a modern classic—especially when paired with David Christiana's lush watercolor illustrations (pictured).

IMAGINEERING THE PERFECT VACATION

Have you ever wondered what it would be like to take a vacation to a Disney theme park with an actual, honest-to-goodness Disney Imagineer? If so, it will be well worth your while to pick up a copy of *The Imagineering Field Guide to the Magic Kingdom at Walt Disney World*. As compiled by Alex Wright from the Imagineers, those creative geniuses behind the design of every one of Disney's theme parks, this portable guidebook contains enough stories, anecdotes, insider details, schematics, and concept art to satisfy even the most hard-core Disney fan, all of it nicely laid out with accompanying illustrations. It's the next best thing to having an Imagineer in tow!

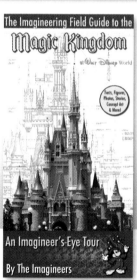

A GLIMPSE INSIDE THE ARCHIVES

In *The Disney Keepsakes*, a handsome new companion volume to *The Disney Treasures*, author Robert Tieman once again digs deep into the Walt Disney Archives. This time around, Tieman delves into the history of Disney during Walt's life, while also filling in the details surrounding the innovative man's many side projects. Organized chronologically and by topic, the book contains several never-before-published facsimiles from the Archives, many of which are removable. If you consider yourself a Disney fan, *The Disney Keepsakes* is a must-have volume.

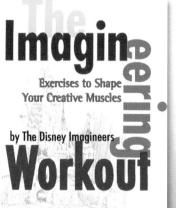

TONE YOUR MENTAL MUSCLE

Almost everyone has ended up in a creative rut at one point or another—even, believe it or not, Disney's fabled Imagineers. To fend off the funk, the men and women of Walt Disney Imagineering have developed a mental regimen that helps keep their creativity in tip-top shape. In *The Imagineering Workout*, longtime Imagineer Peggy Van Pelt, Ph.D., shares the exercises used for the express purpose of stimulating and inspiring Disney's star creative talent. In addition, there are personal insights from Walt Disney Imagineering vice chairman and principal creative executive Marty Sklar and others. With this book, your imagination and creativity will be in top shape in no time at all—guaranteed.

CELEBRATING 50 MAGICAL YEARS

This past year, Disney released two tomes in commemoration of Disneyland's 50th anniversary. *The Art of Disneyland* by Jeff Kurtti and Bruce Gordon chronicles the evolution of Disney's first Magic Kingdom, from Walt Disney Imagineering's initial designs to the finished attractions themselves. The book is filled with large, stunning reproductions of fifty years' worth of Disneyland concept art and covers all areas of the park—from Main Street, U.S.A., to Tomorrowland, as well as more recent additions such as Mickey's Toontown.

Meanwhile, Tim O'Day and Bruce Gordon's *Disneyland Then, Now, and Forever* traces the fifty-year history of Disneyland through text and pictures. Starting with what Disneyland might have been like had it been built as originally intended, next to the Walt Disney Studios in Burbank, the volume goes on to detail the many rides and attractions that have come and gone over the years. Filled with rare color illustrations, behind-the-scenes anecdotes, and before-and-after photographs of the Park's construction and development, it is the perfect companion volume to *The Art of Disneyland*. Both books are available exclusively at the Disney theme parks.

W.I.T.C.H. WAY FOR NEW ADVENTURES

Will, Irma, Taranee, Cornelia, and Hay-Lin—better known as "W.I.T.C.H."—are five seemingly ordinary girls charged with an extraordinary mission: as Guardians of the Veil, they must keep Earth safe from the evil Prince Phobos, ruler of a parallel world called Meridian. The girls' ongoing adventures have been chronicled in a series of popular chapter books, including recent titles *The Courage to Choose*, *Path of Revenge*, *The Darkest Dream*, and *Keeping Hope*. Now, with the introduction of two new series, W.I.T.C.H. Graphic Novels and W.I.T.C.H. Adventures, fans can delve even deeper into their world.

The graphic novels, four-color comics that bear a strong manga influence, are filled with dramatic story lines, battles, and betrayals. W.I.T.C.H. Adventures are original narratives that detail how each girl overcomes obstacles and defeats villains with the help of her friends—learning, in the process, to appreciate her unique powers and special friendship with the others. Watch for the latest graphic novel, *Between Light and Dark*, and the newest book in the W.I.T.C.H. Adventures series, *Enchanted Music*.

AFTER HOURS IN THE MAGIC KINGDOM

Thriller writer Ridley Pearson, who co-authored last year's *Peter and the Starcatchers* with Dave Barry, returns with another exciting book for kids and teens. In *The Kingdom Keepers*, Pearson vividly imagines the goings-on within Magic Kingdom Park at Walt Disney World after closing time. Orlando resident Finn Whitman, one of five teenagers selected to become models for holographic guides at the Park, unexpectedly finds himself inside the Magic Kingdom at night—in holographic form. Caught somewhere between dream and reality, Finn must join with an elderly Imagineer to defend both the Magic Kingdom and the outside world from the evil Maleficent and the Overtakers. Pearson's novel combines high-tech thrills with a deep appreciation for Disney lore, resulting in a book that is sure to appeal to adults and children alike.

PUBLISHING—A LOOK AHEAD

*Disney Publishing Worldwide has several new and exciting titles due out in 2006.
Whether it's a new pirate adventure, another exciting Never Land voyage, or a peek inside the Disney Casting
Department's files, there's bound to be a book to appeal to almost anyone. Here is just a sampling.*

PIRATE ADVENTURE: Jack Sparrow
Before the *Black Pearl* and raving-mad skeletons, there was a teenage stowaway named Jack Sparrow. Beginning Spring 2006, Disney Press will publish an ongoing series of junior novels based on everyone's favorite pirate of the Caribbean—Captain Jack Sparrow—during his wild and venturesome teenage years. The series, written in a style that, like the films, blends the serious and lighthearted, will launch with two volumes and then continue on a bimonthly basis. Each digest-sized novel will be illustrated with five pieces of full-page artwork in an edgy and bold graphic style by the Disney Storybook artists. Covers will be rendered by graphic novel artist John Van Fleet. Each book is a self-contained story that lives within the larger context of a serialized tale.

NEVER LAND RETURNS

Pulitzer Prize–winning humorist Dave Barry and novelist Ridley Pearson continue the adventures begun in *Peter and the Starcatchers*. In their newest book, *Peter and the Shadow Thieves*, Peter, the leader of the Lost Boys, sophisticated Molly, and the orphan crew of the ship *Never Land* return for another round of high-seas adventure and roguish humor. Additionally, Barry and Pearson have co-authored the Never Land Adventures, a new series of chapter books filled with adventures from Mollusk Island. The first two books in the series, *Escape from the Carnivale* and *Cave of the Dark Wind*, along with *Peter and the Shadow Thieves*, will hit bookstores in 2006.

WHAT A BUNCH OF CHARACTERS
Disney Dossiers: Files of Character from the Walt Disney Studios
Direct from the extensive files of the Walt Disney Casting Department in Burbank, California, and assembled for your research and enlightenment, here is a one-of-a-kind collection of Disney "character reference." Offering an entertaining and informative look into the careers of Disney's best-loved animated characters—whether their roles were starring or supporting—*Disney Dossiers* brings together a fascinating collection of information, anecdotes, and illustrations, providing highlights from Disney productions past, and staying current with its present. Lavishly illustrated throughout with rare and never-before-seen artwork and photographs, *Disney Dossiers* will further enrich the reader's appreciation of the varied bunch of characters that have populated Disney's animated films.

DISNEY ONLINE

Disney Online Shines in Cyberspace

This last year was another year of innovation for the Walt Disney Internet Group. For the first time, Toons could find the portal to Toontown Online through boxed CD-ROMs purchased in retail stores—a new way for guests to enter the massively multiplayer online game that lets players form friendships and battle the evil Cogs.

In July, Disney lovers learned that they would soon be able to put their favorites on their phones with the announcement of Disney Mobile. Disney partnered with Sprint, using the Sprint Nationwide PCS Nationwide Network, to create the first national U.S. wireless phone service specifically designed for families. Disney Mobile, slated to launch in 2006, will offer special handsets and mobile phone products with a Disney flair. Families will be able to take advantage of new security and customization features that will put Mom and Dad in charge.

"Podcast" was one of the hottest high-tech buzzwords of the year, and Disney Online was the forefront of the trend. Disneyland Resort produced podcasts in May and June to celebrate the launch of the 50th Anniversary celebration, and Disney Online followed on June 28 with a regular series of podcasts, featuring a variety of stories about "all things Disney." Radio Disney, Disneyland Resort, and Walt Disney World podcast content are all available via the iTunes podcast directory.

For young children and their parents, the big news was the December debut of Preschool Time Online. A groundbreaking educational product for two- to five-year-olds, Preschool Time Online combines TV-quality animation with fun learning content featuring familiar characters from Disney Channel's Preschool Time television shows—all experienced online. Subscribers enjoy biweekly updates starring Bear and his friends.

IN GOOD COMPANY: CONSUMER PRODUCTS

Cinderella's spell doesn't end at midnight

In honor of the first-ever Platinum Edition DVD release of *Cinderella*, Disney has created an unrivaled collection of products for children, fans, and enthusiasts. From toys and consumer electronics to high-end jewelry and home decor, Disney has developed something for virtually every major consumer category. Here are just a few of the innovative *Cinderella*-themed items that arrived in time for the recent holiday season.

Fit for a Princess

Disney partnered with Swarovski to create a dazzling collection of *Cinderella*-inspired designer jewelry. A sharp-eyed look at **Swarovski's Cinderella tiara, bracelet, and choker** reveals that the slipper and coach are subtly incorporated into the design of each piece. The **Swarovski earrings** have a tiny version of Cinderella's slipper set above a pavé heart and clear crystal bead.

Never Late for the Ball

The **Twinkle Lights Cinderella Doll** (*left*) has the heroine's signature blue dress and sparkling glass slippers, both of which light up with the touch of a button. An included magic wand lets anyone play Fairy Godmother.

The **Cinderella Magical Talking Vanity** (*below*) is an interactive toy that lets little girls pretend Cinderella is helping them get ready for the Royal Ball. Using voice-activated software, Cinderella guides children through a range of jewelry and makeup choices, with Cinderella's face appearing in the light-up mirror at the end.

Princesses want to have fun

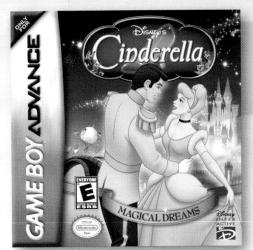

Disney's Cinderella: Magical Dreams, created by Buena Vista Games, the interactive division of Disney, is a side-scrolling action game for the Nintendo Game Boy Advance. The title has multiple levels based on scenes from the movie—from Cinderella doing her chores all the way through to the Royal Ball.

Developed for the PC, **Disney's Cinderella Dollhouse 2** lets children ages four to six help the Fairy Godmother decorate a castle for Cinderella's upcoming parties.

Take the Party Home

The 13-inch **Cinderella TV** (*left*) has a blue and pink cabinet topped with tiara-shaped speakers, while the similarly styled **Cinderella DVD Player** has a custom Disney on-screen user interface. Meanwhile, the **Cinderella Karaoke Player**'s intriguing form factor is meant to resemble the carriage that whisks Cinderella to and from the ball (*right*).

HOLIDAY MAGIC

Feeling nostalgic? Then Disney's holiday decorations are just for you. The new **Best Night of the Week** tree ornament celebrates cozy evenings spent gathered around the TV for *The Wonderful World of Disney*. It's sold at Hallmark Gold Crown stores, as well as select department and drug stores.

You can also relive past memories with the **Legacy of Walt Disney** snow globe. A stack of model sheets serves as the base for five small globes containing Disney's beloved animated characters. In the center is a larger globe holding none other than Mickey Mouse himself. When the base is wound, the characters inside the smaller globes spin to the tune of "A Dream Is a Wish Your Heart Makes." Made of sculpted resin and glass, this hand-painted piece is available from DisneyShopping.com.

CRYSTAL CLEAR: Walt Disney Art Classics and Swarovski have worked together to re-create Disney's most famous characters in crystal. Mickey, Minnie, Donald, Daisy, Goofy, and Pluto are now available as high-quality figurines with subtle Jet crystal accents. They can be purchased at Swarovski retail stores and from swarovski.com.

PERSONAL ELECTRONICS

Just in time for the holiday season, Disney unveiled a new line of cutting-edge electronic devices. Although geared primarily toward children, these items are bound to appeal to all Disney fans, as well as anyone whose taste runs toward the whimsical.

HOME FROM THE HUNDRED ACRE WOOD: Disney's matching **Winnie the Pooh television and DVD player** come encased in yellow and red housings. The new 13-inch television has a Pooh- and Tigger-themed on-screen interface. The DVD player features a Pooh screensaver and offers support for MP3 file playback.

PULLING DOUBLE DUTY: The new **Disney Princess Locket-Style Wearable Digital VGA Camera** *(below)* is both a piece of jewelry and a nifty electronic device. Inside the pink beaded necklace is a compact digital camera capable of taking VGA-resolution (640 x 480) pictures. The locket camera is powered by a built-in rechargeable battery and contains 8 MB of memory for storing up to fifty images.

YES, YOU CAN TAKE IT WITH YOU: Two new devices let everyone enjoy Disney entertainment on the go. Available in four styles, including the sleek looking "Disney Chrome" (pictured), the **Disney Mix Stick** is a PC- and Mac-compatible digital music device that plays both MP3 and Windows Media audio files. Music can be downloaded to the Mix Stick using standard music-downloading software and a USB connection, or songs can be copied from CDs to the device's built-in 128 MB memory (expandable to 1 GB). It is also compatible with the new "Disney Mix Clip" prerecorded music cards.

Meanwhile, the new **Disney Personal DVD Player** is a compact, easy-to-use device that not only plays DVDs and CDs, but JPEG and MP3 files stored on disc. It features integrated speakers, built-in rechargeable batteries, and two headphone jacks (great for sharing digital media with friends and family). The player, which comes in both a handheld version with a 3.5-inch LCD and a larger "clamshell" style with a seven-inch screen, is available in several styles, including "Classic Disney," "Disney Princess," and "Power Rangers."

RETURN OF A CLASSIC

If you like retro, you'll want to check out the newest items in Disney's popular line of Vintage Mickey products. Stitched together from a collection of classic scenes, the Vintage Mickey throw makes for the perfect way to keep warm on a cold night. For the ultimate in form and comfort, be sure to complement the throw with a Vintage Mickey denim pillow. Then, after getting snuggled in for the winter, count down the days till spring with a 2006 Vintage Mickey calendar, available in two sizes. All Vintage Mickey items are available from select specialty retailers.

TOYS

The latest toys from Disney merge the latest technologies with traditional modes of play.
Below are some of the company's cutting-edge creative, interactive, and imaginative products.

PERSONAL CHRONICLES: Now everyone can engage in an ultimate battle of good and evil from the comfort of home. As a tie-in to the holiday release of *The Chronicles of Narnia: The Lion, the Witch and the Wardrobe*, Disney has created the **Deluxe Battle Set**, a collection of seven highly detailed and articulated characters from the armies of Aslan and the White Witch.

LET LOOSE THE CREATIVE MUSE: **The Disney Dreamsketcher** is a handheld activity center that encourages artistic expression. Included software allows kids to draw, color, and play games on the built-in screen using an attached stylus. The device lets children save their artwork for later printing on a PC.

GET MOVIN': Intended to encourage motor skills in young children, the 12.5-inch tall **Tumble Time Tigger** does cartwheels and sings his own theme song, "TiggerTime" (set to the MC Hammer tune "Can't Touch This"). Lovable and huggable, he's sure to delight infants and toddlers—and probably even more than a few adults.

VIDEO GAMES

ENTER THE WARDROBE: Based on the film from Walt Disney Pictures and Walden Media, Buena Vista Games' **The Chronicles of Narnia: The Lion, the Witch and the Wardrobe** takes players into the frozen land of Narnia, where young siblings Peter, Susan, Edmund, and Lucy Pevensie must help Aslan the lion defeat the evil White Witch and her minions. Along the way, gamers will encounter fantastic creatures such as centaurs, minotaurs, minoboars, cyclopses, werewolves, wraiths, satyrs, boggles, and more. Incorporating footage, vocal talent, and music from the film, this multiplatform release lets gamers play all four heroes in a team-based adventure. Both solo and multiplayer game modes are supported.

NOT SO LITTLE: Based on the 3-D–animated film from Walt Disney Pictures, **Disney's Chicken Little** is an action-packed game title set in the town of Oakey Oaks. Gamers play Chicken Little and his misfit friends, Abby Mallard, Runt of the Litter, and Fish out of Water, as they try to outwit town bully Foxy Loxy, save the town from alien invasion, and repair Chicken Little's tarnished reputation. The game features clips, celebrity voices, and 3-D environments from the film, as well as an extended story line. Disney's Chicken Little is available for PlayStation2, Nintendo GameCube, Xbox, Game Boy Advance, and PC.

JACK'S BACK: Buena Vista Games continues the story of Jack Skellington and his nemesis Oogie Boogie with two new software titles. Picking up where the movie left off, **Tim Burton's The Nightmare Before Christmas: Oogie's Revenge** lets players take on the role of Jack, who must stop Oogie Boogie from kidnapping the leaders of all the holidays. This title for PlayStation2 and Xbox has more than twenty-five bizarre levels of game play and a freaky cast of characters, including Dr. Finklestein; the mischievous Lock, Shock, and Barrel; and others.

Tim Burton's The Nightmare Before Christmas: The Pumpkin King for Game Boy Advance is a prequel to the film that explains how Jack Skellington first faced off against Oogie Boogie and became the Pumpkin King. This side-scrolling action title features eerie locations such as Halloween Town Square and Dr. Finklestein's Laboratory.

INSPIRED ENDING FOR
75 INSP-EAR-ATIONS

In September 2005, The Walt Disney Company capped off its celebration of Mickey Mouse's 75th anniversary, "Celebrate Mickey: 75 InspEARations," by auctioning seventy-five unique Mickey statues for charity at Sotheby's in New York City. The statues, which each stand six feet tall and weigh in at more than 700 pounds, were individually designed and decorated by a range of luminaries, including artists, actors, musicians, athletes, and famed Disney legends.

Among the celebrity-designed Mickey statues that commanded a premium at auction were (*above, left to right*) Sir Elton John's "Music Royalty" ($52,000), Michelle Kwan's "Peace & Love" ($20,000), and Tom Hanks' "Space Mouse" ($15,000).

Several statues by current and former Disney cast members were also among the most sought-after items. Disney Legend Al Konetzni's "Back to School" (*left*), for example, brought in $45,000, while statues by Disney Publishing's Lori Tyminski's "Funny Pages" (*below*) and Disney Consumer Products' Tuck Morgan's "Mickey Through the Years" (*right*) together pulled in an additional $50,000. All told, the auction raised some $614,500 for fifty worthwhile charities, including the Make-A-Wish Foundation of America, the Boys and Girls Club of America, the Elizabeth Glaser Pediatric AIDS Foundation, and others.

You may have caught a glimpse of the seventy-five Mickeys during their nationwide twelve-city tour, which began in November 2003 and ended shortly before the Sotheby's auction. If you didn't, Sotheby's has an auction catalog showing the entire collection that can be ordered at www.sothebys.com/mickey. Note that the first 5,000 orders sold include a free, limited-edition commemorative pin featuring the 75th-anniversary Mickey engraved with edition number and sale information.

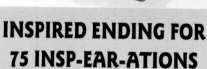

DISNEY GOES 3-D FOR NEW FILM RELEASES

The pioneering multiplane camerawork in films such as *Pinocchio* and *Bambi*, the use of stereo sound for *Fantasia*, the Audio-Animatronics developed for theme park attractions as in Pirates of the Caribbean and The Haunted Mansion—when it comes to using technology as an adjunct to creativity, Disney is always looking for ways to push the envelope. The recent unveiling of Disney Digital 3-D proves to be no exception. Developed in collaboration with Dolby Laboratories, this brand-new, state-of-the-art technology provides the first true three-dimensional digital experience in movie theaters.

Disney Digital 3-D was first used in select venues to enhance the theatrical exhibition of the CG-animated *Chicken Little*. Industrial Light & Magic, George Lucas's famed visual-effects company, utilized a proprietary process to render the film in a 3-D format. When this new format is projected in theaters equipped with the new Dolby Digital Cinema system and viewed using a new breed of stereoscopic glasses, it achieves a stunning level of verisimilitude unlike anything seen before. In the case of *Chicken Little*, the 3-D enhancement makes the film's colorful, stylized design seem to pop off the screen.

For *Chicken Little*'s opening, Disney Digital 3-D was rolled out in 84 high-profile theaters nationwide, including Disney's flagship El Capitan Theatre in Hollywood. Expect to see it become more widely available in the near future, such as next December's *Meet the Robinsons*.

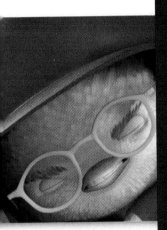

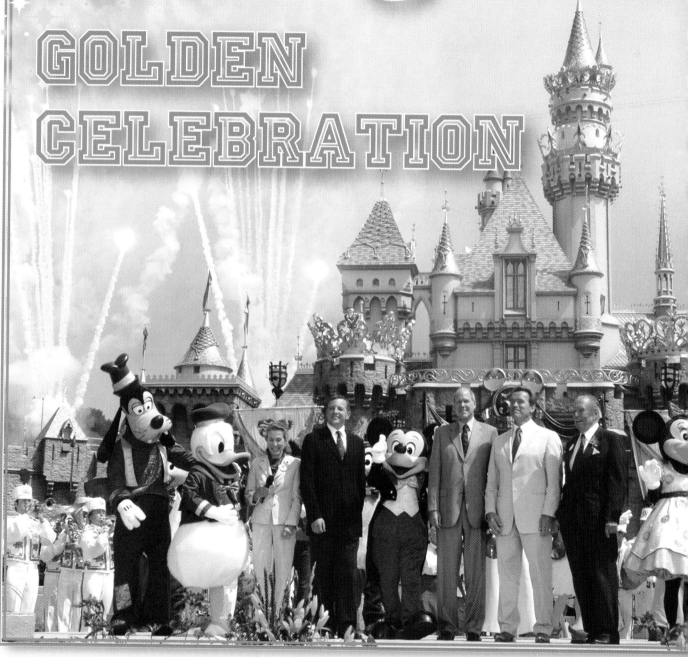

Disneyland

GOLDEN CELEBRATION

The Roots of Disneyland

by Rebecca Cline

Reality is complicated. Myth is tidy.

The evolution of Disneyland is archetypal "Disney": the coming together of diverse and unlikely concepts into a revolutionary entertainment form. Like many Disney innovations, Disneyland did not happen because that is what Walt Disney set out to do. The links in Disneyland's evolutionary chain go all the way back to Walt's rural boyhood and extend forward through his professional and personal life.

Walt himself never liked intellectual analysis of his work, and he would simply summarize each important professional or creative circumstance in a defining anecdote or story. In that way, over the years, Walt came to define Disneyland's origin this way:

"Well, it came about when my daughters were very young. Saturday was always Daddy's day with the two daughters. So we'd start out and try to go someplace, and I'd take 'em to the merry-go-round and took 'em different places. And as I'd sit there while they rode the merry-go-round, did all these things, sat on a bench, eating peanuts, I felt that there should be something built, some kind of amusement enterprise built where the parents and the children could have fun together. So that's how Disneyland started."

Now, while this is not a myth, or a made-up story, it is only one component of Disneyland's evolution, and it is as interesting for the elements it omits as for those it contains.

Walt had always been a fan of circuses, carnivals, and fairs. Disney executive Joe Fowler once said, "Walt was always wanting to go to these places. Every summer, Walt would send me to Europe for ideas. Often he would come along. We'd go to world's fairs, Oktoberfests, gardens, amusement parks—you

ABOVE: Walt Disney was fascinated with building, construction, and how things work. Here, he gets an insider's view of an under-construction Disneyland circus wagon.

name it." Walt had created a custom Mickey Mouse cartoon *Mickey's Surprise Party* for the 1939 New York World's Fair and had been an enthusiastic visitor to the "other" 1939 fair, the Golden Gate International Exposition in San Francisco. Some of the things Walt saw there, and returned with, were meticulously handcrafted miniatures. A few years later, when stress caused Walt's doctor to advise him to find a hobby, Walt began to design and handcraft miniatures of his own.

Having grown up in the American Midwest, Walt was always entranced by the power and romance of railroading. As a teen, he had been a "news butcher," selling newspapers, peanuts, and candy on the Missouri Pacific Railroad out of Kansas City. At the suggestion of Studio nurse Hazel George, Walt attended the 1948 Chicago Railroad Fair with animator Ward Kimball, and the two rail fans had a wonderful time riding the legendary locomotives on display. Afterwards, they visited Henry Ford's Edison Institute Museum and Historical Greenfield Village located in Dearborn, Michigan. Walt was deeply impressed with the historic buildings, and most of all with the vintage train chuffing around the property. Soon after his return, he combined his miniature-making hobby with his love of trains.

In September of 1948, under the tutelage of machinist Roger Broggie, Walt became an apprentice in his own Studio machine shop. The two began building an inch-and-a-half scale, seven-and-a-quarter-inch gauge 1870s-style locomotive. Although a great deal of the work was done by machinists and craftsmen at the Studio, Walt did much of it himself, and the new engine was christened the *Lilly Belle* in honor of Lillian Disney, his wife.

On June 1, 1949, Walt and Lillian bought a new home at 355 Carolwood Drive in Holmby Hills, and Walt began planning the *Carolwood Pacific*, a miniature live-steam railroad to run around the property. The train had its first trial run on Christmas eve 1949, in Studio Stage 1, and was soon circling 2,600 feet of track, including a 40-foot timber trestle, 2 tunnels, and a perfectly scaled and manicured landscape at his home.

However burdensome it might have been for him at times, the Studio he completed in Burbank in 1940 had another unexpected creative blessing for Walt. He threw himself into every detail of its design and execution, just as he had with his filmmaking endeavors. He contemplated Studio tours, but couldn't imagine anything duller than watching people make movies, especially animated ones. Still, he kept receiving requests from kids who wanted to see where Mickey Mouse and Snow White lived, and shortly thereafter he mentioned

to animator Ben Sharpsteen that he was thinking of creating displays of Disney characters in their fantasy surroundings on land adjacent to the Studio, so that visitors might see something more than "just people working." Imagineer John Hench remembers looking out the window and seeing Walt, a lone figure in the distance, pacing off the wasted sliver of land between the Studio and the Los Angeles Flood Control Channel.

In 1948, Walt circulated a memo about his "kiddie park" idea with detailed descriptions of what would eventually become Main Street, U.S.A., Frontierland, and "a carnival section with roller coasters and merry-go-rounds." A short while later he hired art director Harper Goff to begin working on top secret plans and drawings for his new park.

In the 1950s, these concepts began to amalgamate as Walt began yet another, separate project, known variously as "Walt Disney's America" and "Disneylandia," which would tour the country. Walt asked animator Ken Anderson to design a scale-model American town, whose buildings could house Walt's collection of miniatures in a proper setting. He told Ken "I'm tired of all of you [artists] doing all the drawing and painting around here. You know, I can draw and paint myself. I'm going to do something creative, too. I'm putting you in a private room and taking you off the payroll; I'll pay you out of my own pocket. I want you to draw some typical scenes in miniature. When we get enough of them made, it will travel all over the United States. It will be like a little labyrinth, and when you break an electric eye the models will come to life."

Walt planned to tour the exhibit by creating traveling exhibit train baggage cars that would tour the country with platforms for people to get on and off.

Walt set Ken up in a little workroom in the Animation Building for which only the two of them had keys, and Ken drew twenty-four scenes. The first scene was dubbed "Project Little Man" and was a one-eighth-inch miniature of an Opera House stage featuring a dancing man. Walt carved one head for

ABOVE: Walt Disney's fascination with miniatures—both animated and static—would ultimately become a key inspiration for the creation of Disneyland.

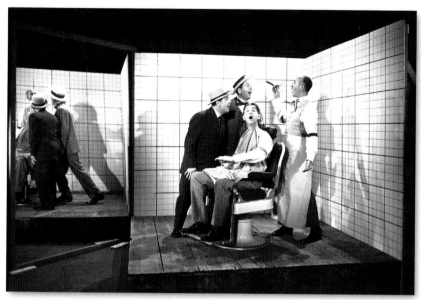

TOP: Reference film was shot of The King's Men singing group performing as a barbershop quartet, as Walt—always searching for a new way to entertain and engage—sought to add movement and music to the miniature scenes he was creating.

CENTER LEFT: Veteran performer Buddy Ebsen (soon to have his career renewed when Walt cast him as Davy Crockett's sidekick Georgie Russel) hoofs under Walt's direction in a reference film shot for Project Little Man.

CENTER RIGHT: One of Walt's first animated miniatures, seen in its primitive early form.

BOTTOM: Busts sculpted by Cristadoro for Project Little Man, the genesis of Disney's Audio-Animatronics technology.

the project by himself but didn't have time to do much else, so he hired sculptor Charles Cristadoro to carve the jointed, nine-inch figure. Wathel Rogers and Roger Broggie were brought in to design a system of cams to make the figure move.

Walt asked actor and former vaudeville hoofer Buddy Ebsen to come to the Studio to tap dance in front of a grid pattern while being filmed. After analyzing the film, Broggie and Rogers were able to reproduce Ebsen's movements for the mechanical dancing figure. While the small group of technicians were working on the "dancing man," and a second figure "the drunkard," Walt took one sketch himself and built a diorama of "Granny's Cabin," based on a set from the 1949 Disney feature film *So Dear to My Heart*. Walt reproduced the set in miniature and planned to build a figure of the grandmother sitting in a rocking chair, sewing a quilt, and telling stories about her life.

Harper Goff designed a third, more elaborate scene—a barbershop quartet with figures that would not only move, but would sing "Down by the Old Mill Stream" in harmony. Live-action filming was done, and Walt built the set in great detail while Cristadoro built the figures in the machine shop and Goff's wife, Flossie, made clothes for the figures.

In the first practical test of Walt's traveling show, "Granny's Cabin" was displayed at the "Festival of Living" show at the Pan Pacific Auditorium in Los Angeles in 1952. Actress Beulah Bondi, the original Granny Kincaid in the film, recorded a narration that played when the lights went on. Although the display was well received, Walt realized that the idea of a traveling rail exhibit was not cost-effective, would have a low visitor capacity, and had far too many technical problems to overcome, so he abruptly told his staff to shelve everything. He had decided upon a much grander scheme.

On March 27, 1952, the first public announcement of Walt Disney's plans to build a park were printed in the *Burbank Daily Review* with the headline, "Walt Disney Make-Believe Land Project Planned Here." By the summer of 1953, Walt had engaged the Stanford Research Institute to find a bigger property of the right size and in the right location. Everything from his first visit to the circus as a child to his last trip around his backyard railroad had, at last, culminated in the undertaking that Walt would call "Disneyland."

So you see, what we know today as Disneyland had a gestation of nearly half a century. It's just not very tidy storytelling. So, for posterity, Disneyland was simply a "magical little park" that grew out of the desire of a weary father with two young daughters in tow, who merely wanted "an amusement enterprise built where the parents and the children could have fun together."

Because reality is complicated. Myth is tidy.

Go to

www.Disney.com/DisneyInsider

Fifty 50s

50 WAYS TO SPOT A GOLDEN ANNIVERSARY

by Tim O'Day

Guests visiting the Disneyland Resort in California during its eighteen-month 50th anniversary celebration are sure to enjoy the many new innovative attractions and entertainment spectaculars that premiered at "The Happiest Place on Earth" as part of its milestone event.

However, ardent Disney fans and casual, inquisitive guests alike are sure to find fun in spotting a special collection of mini-salutes to the Park's golden anniversary.

Known as the "Hidden 50s," these iconic logos of yellow-gold and deep royal blue are fashioned from the familiar three circles of Mickey's silhouette, with the main circle encasing a large numeral 50. Created specifically for the anniversary, there are not coincidently fifty of these "Hidden 50s" carefully placed throughout the Park.

The "Hidden 50s" continue a tradition of "plussing" that Walt Disney started with Disneyland back in 1955—the notion of adding an extra layer of detail or whimsy that adds to the overall story or experience. Through the years, Disney Imagineers past and present have engaged in the act of "plussing," from the distinctive Main Street windows (fictitious second-story window advertisements that salute key contributors to the Disney parks) to hidden salutes to Mickey to the truly obscure (tongue-in-cheek nods to attractions of the past found in such current-day favorites as The Many Adventures of Winnie the Pooh, Splash Mountain, and Star Tours).

"Disneyland has experienced five decades of constant change and innovation, creating a park rich in detail, history, legend, and lore," says Sayre Weisman of Disneyland Resort Entertainment who led the team responsible for creating the anniversary decor and the "Hidden 50s" concept. "Die-hard Disneyland fans have unearthed many of the Park's secrets through the years and we thought that the concept of the 'Hidden 50s' was just something fun to create for both the fan and the everyday guest."

In developing the "Hidden 50s" concept, Weisman and her team realized that each logo had to be easily seen and identifiable from the Park's many pathways, therefore restricting the placement of the "50s" within attraction interiors of any kind. The "50s" range in size from very large (The Haunted Mansion) to very small (Mr. Toad's Wild Ride). The very first "50" can be found as Guests enter Disneyland and see the new design for the familiar "Flower Mickey" in front of the Main Street Train Station.

"The '50s' were specifically designed to blend in with the art direction of each individual land," states Weisman. "Created from a variety of materials, we have '50s' that appear to be carved, aged, painted, metal—whatever thematically works with its environment."

The location of the "50s" may change throughout the celebration, but rest assured, there are always fifty on display. During the 2005 holiday season, the traditional Christmas tree in Town Square on Main Street, U.S.A., received the "Midas touch" by being resplendent in all-gold ornaments and lights reflecting the 50th anniversary. To top it off, literally, the tree sported a not-so-hidden "50," shimmering with hand-applied 14kt gold leaf!

Although Disneyland Guests can receive a complete list of the "Hidden 50s" daily at City Hall on Main Street, *The Disney Insider Yearbook* is pleased to present this guide to the Disneyland 50th Anniversary "Hidden 50s."

1 – 13 Main Street, U.S.A., Street Lamps
Each real gas street lamp on Main Street sports a "50."
The lamps are over 150 years old and were purchased in
Baltimore, Maryland.

14 Flower Mickey
For fifty years this spot has been one of the most photographed locales in the world. This "50" is fashioned
completely out of real flowers.

15 Main Street Station—Main Entrance
The iconic structure sports a "50" directly above its
venerable clock.

16 Main Street Station—Main Street
The clock tower of the station, facing Town Square,
features a "50".

17 Main Street Opera House
This "50" is placed prominently at the entrance to the
new attraction Disneyland: The First "50" Magical Years.

18 Main Street City Hall
A "50" is perched high above Town Square on the cupola
of City Hall.

19 Sleeping Beauty Castle
Bejeweled for the 50th anniversary, the castle wears
a shining "50" directly above the Disney family coat of
arms that adorns the castle drawbridge entrance.

20 Sleeping Beauty Castle Courtyard
As guests exit the castle, they can spy a small "50"
between two coat-of-arms directly above the archway.

21 Walt Disney's Enchanted Tiki Room
This carved "50" adjacent to the lanai is possibly hard to
find among the lush foliage of Adventureland.

22 Jungle Cruise
Under the attraction marquee, this "50" is literally skew-
ered with native spears and has a faded, aged look.

23 Frontierland Stockade
Just inside the Frontierland stockade entrance, this "50"
can be found among assorted U.S. Cavalry supplies.

24 Frontierland Shootin' Exposition
Placed as part of the attraction marquee, this "50" has
been accidentally riddled with buckshot by a not-so-
sharp shooter.

25 Frontierland Indian
A hand-carved wooden sculpture of a noble American
Indian, replete with feathered headdress and red robe, is
also adorned with a "50" pendant around his neck.

**26 Big Thunder Mountain Railroad
Water Tower**
This "50" is literally painted upon the old plank-board
water tower that supplies water to the mighty runaway
trains of Big Thunder Mountain Railroad

27 Mark Twain Riverboat
This small "50" can be spotted adorning the pilot house
of this majestic vessel. In 1955, the *Mark Twain* riverboat
was the first paddle wheeler built in the United States in
half a century.

28 | Tom Sawyer Island
Harper's Mill features a "50" nailed to the wall along with various metal tubs and pans. The mill acts as the stage backdrop for the nightly spectacular Fantasmic!

29 | Indiana Jones™ Adventure
Literally hanging in rope mesh off the attraction marquee, this "50" appears to be carved of wood and aged to blend-in with the archaeological dig occurring at the base of the Temple of the Forbidden Eye.

30 | Pirates of the Caribbean
This "50" is located directly above the entrance to possibly the most popular Disney theme park adventure of all time, and the direct inspiration for the hit film *Pirates of the Caribbean: Curse of the Black Pearl* and its sequel *Pirates of the Caribbean: Dead Man's Chest*.

31 | New Orleans Square Street Banner
Located above the elegant courtyards and winding streets of this charming area of Disneyland, this "50" themes with the surrounding Mardi Gras décor.

32 | New Orleans Square Balcony
This "50" adorns the entrance to one of the most popular of the many quaint courtyards that guests can find and explore within New Orleans Square.

33 | Sailing Ship Columbia
The figurehead of this unique attraction wears a "50" around her neck. When the ship was built it was the first three-masted windjammer built in the United States in more than one hundred years.

34 | Sailing Ship Columbia (Stern)
An all-gold "50" can be seen under the windows of the Captain's Quarters on the ship. The Sailing Ship *Columbia* is modeled upon the first American vessel to circumnavigate the globe.

35 | The Haunted Mansion
The most unique of the "Hidden 50s" is to be found at the entrance to The Haunted Mansion where the numeral "50" has been fashioned to resemble an oversized spider web.

36 | Splash Mountain
A "50" is carved into the mountain directly below the summit of Chickapin Hill and directly adjacent to the final fifty-two-foot drop into the briar patch below.

37 | Critter Country Train Trestle
A wood-carved "50" decorates this sturdy overpass that carries the authentic steam engines of the Disneyland Railroad.

38 | Frontierland Stagecoach
The stagecoach at Big Thunder Ranch sports a shiny "50" on top of its carriage. The stagecoach was a popular mode of transportation in Frontierland from 1955–1959.

39 | Pinocchio's Daring Journey (Weather Vane)
A "Hidden 50" acts as a weather vane atop this Fantasyland attraction. Other fanciful weather vanes adorn the roofline of Peter Pan's Flight, featuring the Crocodile and Captain Hook's pirate galleon.

40 | Mr. Toad's Wild Ride
A statue of J. Thaddeus Toad that once held a monocle now features "Toady" holding a "Hidden 50."

41 | Mad Tea Party (Lanterns)
One of the yellow Chinese lanterns that hang above the swirling cups and saucers features a "Hidden 50."

42 | Matterhorn Bobsled (Entrance Crest)
As guests approach the chalet to board their bobsleds, they pass right under this "50" nestled among various alpine crests.

43 | Astro Orbitor
Sharp eyes will find one of the swirling and undulating planets of this out-of-this world attraction featuring a hard-to-find "50."

44 | Observatron
One of the futuristic satellite dishes of this "public art" features yet another hard-to-find "50."

45 | Honey, I Shrunk the Audience
A "50" is prominently placed right in the middle of the logo for the imaginary Imagination Institute.

46 | Innoventions
This hard-to-find "50" is featured as part of the decor for one of the loading stages of the rotating attraction.

47 | "it's a small world"
Directly under the beloved attraction's smiling glockenspiel clock is a golden "50," guarding the facade doors where every fifteen minutes a parade of little dolls emerge to announce the time.

48 | Roger Rabbit's Car Toon Spin
At the attraction entrance, Lenny the Cab balances a "50" atop his hood ornament.

49 | Mickey's Toontown Station
A "50" adorns the marquee signage of this station for the Disneyland Railroad.

50 | Mickey's House—Mickey's Toontown
The front entrance to Mickey's residence features a hanging "50" directly over the front door.

Walt Disney Studios

Disneyland's Workshop

by Rebecca Cline

Walt Disney once famously said:
"My only hope is that we never lose sight of one thing—
that it was all started by a mouse."

With the birth of Mickey Mouse in 1928, the Walt Disney Studios in Hollywood felt the need for expansion. Here was a character that had taken the world by storm, and new buildings and stages needed to be constructed to house a growing stable of beloved animated characters and a new style of cartoon short called the "Silly Symphonies." The success of one particular "Silly Symphony," *Three Little Pigs*, gave the fledgling studio the financial wherewithal to begin working on the first ever full-length animated feature film, *Snow White and the Seven Dwarfs*.

It was the financial success of *Snow White* that enabled the Disneys to build an even larger state-of-the-art film and animation studio over the Hollywood Hills in Burbank, California, in 1939. The move was completed in 1940, and almost immediately the Studio began to receive requests from the public for tours of the new plant. Letters poured in from children who wanted to come and see where Mickey Mouse and Snow White lived, and it got Walt to thinking. In a 1956 interview he said, "When I built the Studio over there I thought, Well, gee, we ought to have a three-dimension thing that people could actually come and visit. They can't visit our Studio because the rooms are small. It's too disrupting to have anybody on the lot. So I had a little dream for Disneyland adjoining the Studio."

Walt's little dream went through a number of incarnations through the years. At first, he thought of creating displays of Disney characters in their fantasy surroundings on land adjacent to the new studio, so that visitors might see more than "people just working." His ideas grew more and more elaborate in the ensuing years, and with the development of new personal interests in miniatures and scale-model live-steam trains, his plans for a "kiddie park" evolved into what we know today as Disneyland.

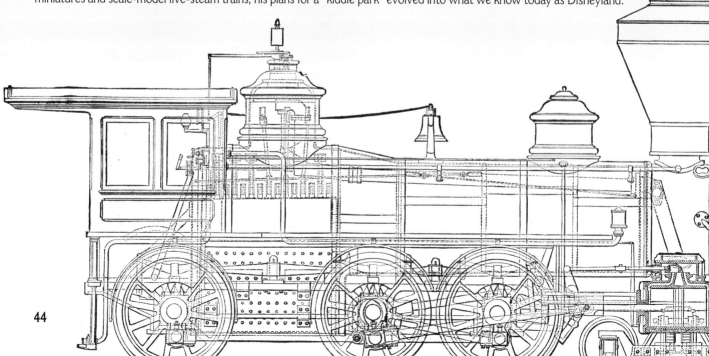

OPPOSITE, BOTTOM: This plan for the train engine of Walt's personal scale-model railroad was made available to other train buffs in 1950.

TOP: Building a building: the Animation Building under construction at the new Disney studio lot in Burbank, 1939.

CENTER: Aerial view of the Disney Studios, including (at far right) the Riverside Drive property that Walt first considered as the site for Disneyland.

BOTTOM: Walt and some lucky passengers take the Disneyland stagecoach for its first run through the streets of the Disney Studios, 1953.

Always the entrepreneur, in 1950 Walt Disney began recovering some of the investment costs of his railroad hobby by informally establishing a private company he called the Walt Disney Miniature Railroad Company. Available to train buffs for purchase were drawings and plans for Walt's backyard locomotive, the *Lilly Belle*, parts castings for engines and cars, and even castings of a miniature potbellied stove that Walt had made for the caboose of his train. Shortly thereafter, in 1952, Walt's private little company was incorporated as WED Enterprises, Inc. (an acronym for Walter Elias Disney). The basic reason for incorporating was to protect Walt's valuable name, but with the creation of WED, Walt was also able to make his amusement park dreams a reality. "Well, WED is, you might call it my backyard laboratory, my workshop away from work," Walt said in a 1964 interview. "It served a purpose in that some of the things I was planning, like Disneyland for example...it's pretty hard for banking minds to go with it...so I had to go ahead on my own and develop it to a point where they could begin to comprehend what I had on my mind."

Early in 1953, Richard Irvine and Marvin Davis, two art directors from 20th Century Fox, joined WED Enterprises. Under Walt's supervision, they begin to gather together a staff to work on the new park. Initially, negotiations were carried out with the architectural firm of Pereira & Luckman to create the overall design of the park, but Irvine and a number of other friends convinced Walt that the park he was describing was not a conventional architectural project. It was their opinion that Walt Disney and his own studio staff were the only ones who could turn his dreams into reality.

In addition to Irvine and Davis, art directors from other motion picture companies were hired to join with Disney studio artists already working for Walt on an early three-dimensional animation project called "Disneylandia." By 1954, the WED staff consisted of designers, architects, writers, artists, sculptors, engineers, special effects artists, model makers, and the masters of many other disciplines—in a blend of talent that was unparalleled in the history of the entertainment industry. As Walt Disney and his new "Imagineers" planned Disneyland, they made use of storytelling methods perfected during decades of motion

picture production. They used storyboards (a technique pioneered by Walt in the creation of his animated shorts) and forced perspective (a long tradition in theatrical set design) to assist them in developing each attraction and in the overall layout of the Park.

As 1953 stretched into 1954, many top background, layout, and scenic artists employed by Walt Disney Productions were asked to join WED for special assignments. For Snow White's Adventures, Mr. Toad's Wild Ride, and Peter Pan's Flight in Fantasyland, artists were called upon to add the "Disney touch" acquired through twenty years of Disney cartooning and animation. Bill Martin and Ken Anderson designed these early Disneyland "dark rides," and the vehicles were built by an outside engineering company, Arrow Development, in Mountain View, California. "Viewing the film was part of the design process," said Martin. "I made the track layout to start with, but we went through storyboards galore. Since the point was to convert Walt's cartoon films to rides in Fantasyland, those dark rides were developed from the original 4' x 8' storyboards and concept sketches made for the animated films." The rides were then mocked up on Studio soundstages because the prefabricated buildings they were setting up to house the dark rides had not yet been installed along both sides of the Sleeping Beauty Castle courtyard.

Things didn't always go smoothly, though, when it came time to install the attractions at the Park. Mr. Toad's Wild Ride was built at the Studio in flats and painted by background artist Claude Coats. Sections of wall, floor, and track were then dismantled and trucked to Anaheim. When they were installed at the Park, Ken Anderson found that something had gone wrong—the plans were sixteen inches off. Fortunately the ride was eighteen inches smaller than the building, but it still required many changes. Anderson liked to joke that assembling the flats was "somewhat akin to building a house of cards with each card weighing five hundred pounds."

The earliest completed attraction designed for the new park was the Frontierland Stagecoach. The stagecoaches helped ignite the enthusiasm for Disneyland around the back lot of the Studio in 1954 and in many ways established the basic approach toward the Park itself. From the very beginning, Walt demanded as much quality as possible in each new attraction. "When Walt first started talking about those stagecoaches, people advised him not to bother with real leather seats or painstakingly carved woodwork," Imagineer John Hench

OPPOSITE, TOP: Walt in the Studio machine shop at work on the miniature train that he would name the *Lilly Belle* in honor of his wife.

OPPOSITE, INSET: The logo for WED (Walter Elias Disney) Enterprises, today known as Walt Disney Imagineering. WED was the company Walt established for the design and construction of Disneyland.

OPPOSITE, CENTER: Backdrops for the Fantasyland Mr. Toad "dark ride" in progress on a Studio soundstage.

BOTTOM: The miniature potbellied stove created by Walt for the caboose of his scale-model railroad.

THIS PAGE, TOP AND MIDDLE: Two Disneyland icons—a railroad locomotive and the *Mark Twain* riverboat—under construction at the Disney Studios.

TOP: This Disney Studios soundstage became a "roundhouse" of sorts as it was home to the under-construction Santa Fe & Disneyland Railroad train cars.

CENTER: Walt and an unidentified Studio staffer examine Disneyland animal figures in the Studio Paint Shop.

BOTTOM: At the Studio, Walt examines carvings for the Disneyland circus wagons.

recalled, "They said people would just carve their initials in the wood and rip the leather anyway. Walt contended that people would respect something well done, a work of art. You might say he 'compromised' to this extent: he insisted only on two things, complete authenticity and perfection!"

By the spring of 1958, the Studio machine shop had evolved from a small movie studio mechanical fabrication and repair shop to a booming factory. The shop was overflowing with Disneyland engineering and mechanization projects under the direction of master machinist Roger Broggie and his staff. In this building, where all of the Studio's huge original animation production cameras were designed, built, and maintained, WED built and refurbished all of the early attractions for the new theme park. "I was still working special effects at the Studio," Broggie remembered. "Walt said…'you're off of this special effects work here. Now we're going to turn this machine shop into a manufacturing facility for Disneyland.'" Thereafter, most of the Park's vehicles, including automobiles, boats, trams, buses, and streetcars were designed by studio engineers and built, one by one, entirely by hand. It was also in the machine shop that Disneyland's steam locomotives, the original monorail system, and the mechanized figures of the Jungle Cruise and Nature's Wonderland were built. In 1962, Audio-Animatronics was developed here for projects that became Great Moments with Mr. Lincoln and "it's a small world."

Quickly running out of working space, the machine shop needed even more elbow room than their quarters could provide, and the Disneyland project overflowed onto the Studio's huge motion picture soundstages and back lot. In these film production soundstages the upper structure of the *Mark Twain* was built; railroad cars, monorails, submarines, and circus wagons were constructed; flying elephants, caterpillars, and phantom boats were fabricated; carousel horses and giant squid were refurbished; and multiple attractions, including the Enchanted Tiki Room, The Haunted Mansion, the Carousel of Progress, and "it's a small world," were mocked up for Walt's inspection. "It must have been quite a sight for movie studio visitors to find the surrounding streets filled with Autopia cars, railroad cars and locomotives, animated animals, and all sorts of 'gags' under construction," recalls Imagineer Bob Gurr.

Another important building on the lot was the model shop. It was here that the original models of the Park were built for Walt to present to Disneyland investors and to show the public on television. It was also here that working models of nearly every new attraction were built, from the *Mark Twain* to the Matterhorn Bobsleds. Once a ride had been storyboarded and concept sketches approved, detailed renderings were painted, showing each building and figure. From these renderings, precise plans were generated and models were fabricated, primarily in wood and fiberglass. Here full-scale models were sculpted for the Jungle Cruise and Nature's Wonderland, and the charming miniature buildings of the Storybook Land Canal Boats were constructed. The model shop's talented artists created devils, fairies, mermaids, and dwarfs for the dark rides; treasure chests and sea serpents for the Submarine Voyage; and many other unique items scattered throughout Walt's "Magic Kingdom."

In 1961, WED Imagineers began to develop a dinner show that would eventually become the first Disneyland attraction to feature a new science called Audio-Animatronics, Walt Disney's Enchanted Tiki Room. The creation of this remarkable system marked the beginning of a new era for WED Enterprises. The advent of the 1964–65 New York World's Fair, which showcased four new Disney attractions featuring these high tech figures, provided a substantial business opportunity, and an exciting creative challenge. WED Enterprises was soon the most active independent designer creating shows and exhibits for New York's gigantic international exposition.

By the mid-1960s the Studio was bursting from lack of space, not only in terms of equipment but also for accommodating personnel. The grounds were trying to contain all the workload of the motion pictures, television, publications, and recordings, as well as new attractions for Disneyland, and the very technologically advanced projects that were being developed for the Fair. "We have to have more room!" exclaimed Walt. "The World's Fair is not the Disney Studio—it's WED. We are just going to have to separate and get off the lot."

In 1965, they discovered all the space they would need at the Grand Central Industrial Park in nearby Glendale, California, and some of the departments moved off the lot. An amazing era at the Walt Disney Studio ended, and a new world of Imagineering began.

Walt himself put it this way: "Look at Disneyland. That was started because we had the talents to start it, the talents of the organization. And our World's Fair shows—what we did was possible only because we already had the staff that had worked together for years, blending creative ideas with technical know–how. See, actually, though people don't realize it, Disneyland is designed by the same staff that has done *Snow White* and all the pictures. I have that reservoir of talent that I can draw on, and that's why, when people talk about making another Disneyland, they better first see what reservoir of talent they have to draw on like I have."

So Disneyland was started by a mouse … and three pigs … and seven dwarfs … and a potbellied stove. 🐭

Walt Disney's Fantasyland
From the Movies to the Magic Kingdom

by Jason Surrell

"**Y**ou know, it's a shame people come to Hollywood and find there's nothing to see," Walt Disney told animator Ward Kimball in the late 1940s. Disneyland may have been partly born of Walt Disney's desire to build "a new kind of amusement enterprise" to enjoy with his daughters, a place where children and adults could have fun together, but the Magic Kingdom was also directly inspired by Walt's long-held interest in enabling visitors to Hollywood to really "see something." Even visiting the seemingly exciting set of a live-action film was—and is—ultimately about as interesting as watching ink and paint dry. Walt wanted to give his audience nothing less than the opportunity to step into a motion picture for themselves, to actually live the stories that they had heretofore passively observed on a movie screen. That's what Disneyland was—and is—ultimately about: three-dimensional storytelling. Living the story. Living the adventure. And Fantasyland in particular is all about living the fantasy of Walt Disney's classic animated features.

To bring his movies to life in the real world, Walt turned not to traditional architects and engineers but to actual filmmakers, knowing they were

the only ones who could effectively transport an audience to another time and place, just as they had been doing for years on-screen. The freshly minted "Imagineers" screened Walt's animated features in search of ideas for both walk-through and ride-through attractions for the Park, from the very first one, *Snow White and the Seven Dwarfs*, to the film that was then in production, *Sleeping Beauty*. Expanding upon the notion of Disneyland as a three-dimensional film, the Imagineers drew storyboards for the attractions just as they would for the latest animated feature, envisioning each ride, scene-by-scene, from beginning to end. Walt himself led the creative charge, describing the entire Snow White attraction for his Imagineers just as he had pitched the film version to his animators on an empty soundstage more than twenty years before.

As the Imagineers continued to dream and draw these living animated features, veteran Disney writer-producer Bill Walsh described Disneyland in detail for the first time in a written treatment. As Bill wrote, Fantasyland was to be located "within the walls of a great medieval castle, with a King Arthur carousel, Snow White ride-through, Alice in Wonderland walk-through, and Peter Pan fly-through."

Fantasyland was first designed to be an enchanting miniature village that would make Guests truly feel as though they had stepped into a frame of one of Walt's animated feature films. But thanks to time constraints and budget cuts, the WED team was forced to "value imagineer" the elaborate castle courtyard Walt had envisioned into a collection of medieval festival facades and tournament tents, a less costly and decidedly less whimsical alternative to his original fairy tale village.

Architect and Imagineer Bill Martin recalled how WED's creative solution enabled them to create some semblance of a quaint European village square: "We decided to use festive tournament tents on the attraction entrances. It still kept the village atmosphere, while being quite cost-effective."

While the result was more than magical enough for Guests, the Imagineers weren't fooling themselves—or Walt. When the Storybook Land Canal Boats opened in 1956, it quickly became obvious that that attraction, with its charming miniature castles, winding cobblestone streets, and curlicue storybook architecture, represented Walt's true vision for "the happiest land of all." It would be almost thirty years before the same royal treatment could be applied to the rest of Fantasyland during a complete redesign in 1983.

ABOVE: The original "festive tournament tent" facade of Mr. Toad's Wild Ride.

BELOW: Disney characters—including holiday favorites, the wooden soldiers from Walt Disney's *Babes in Toyland*—celebrate in front of Sleeping Beauty Castle, circa Christmas 1961.

OPPOSITE: Sleeping Beauty Castle rises above the Disneyland site. Walt instructed that Sleeping Beauty Castle be among the first structures built, so that its presence would serve as an inspiration for the construction of the rest of Disneyland.

The star attractions of Fantasyland were the "dark rides," so called because they took place indoors and were theatrically lit with black light, ultraviolet illumination that made the fluorescent paint on the scenery and animated figures glow in the dark. The three original dark rides were Mr. Toad's Wild Ride, suggested by the "Wind in the Willows" segment of 1949's *The Adventures of Ichabod and Mr. Toad*; Peter Pan Flight (later renamed Peter Pan's Flight), based on *Peter Pan* (1953); and Snow White's Adventures (later more accurately titled Snow White's Scary Adventures), inspired by Walt's first animated feature, *Snow White and the Seven Dwarfs* (1937).

Art director Ken Anderson had worked on most of the films upon which the Fantasyland attractions were based, but he quickly realized that telling these classic stories in three dimensions was a completely different proposition. Ken knew that guests would be moving quickly through each scene in a mine car, motorcar, or pirate ship, so they'd have neither the time nor the concentration required to really "get" the story or relate to the characters like they would if they were watching it all unfold on a movie screen. Since they couldn't get away with telling a literal and linear narrative, Ken decided to focus instead on the powerful emotions elicited by the physical environments in which the stories took place.

All three of the chosen film properties were well suited to this particular creative approach. Snow White's Adventures was perfect for the dark-ride treatment, not because of its timeless story or beloved characters, but thanks to the sheer diversity and richness of its settings: the Seven Dwarfs' Alpine country cottage and sparkling diamond mine, the Queen's forbidding castle dungeon and, as the attraction's chilling centerpiece, the Dark Forest. The exotic world of Peter Pan was a natural because it enabled guests to experience the unique—for an amusement park ride—sensation of flight, a quality that even makes it unique in the world and guarantees a long wait time for the attraction at almost any hour of the day. And Mr. Toad's Wild Ride plunged riders into the unbridled chaos of a madcap jaunt from stately Toad Hall to the depths of hell itself. An attraction based on a film set in the ultimate fantasy environment, Alice in Wonderland, was initially planned for opening day, but Walt's longtime nemeses, time and money, delayed the attraction's addition until 1958.

With such alluring "locations" to work with, the Imagineers kept the stories themselves relatively simple and designed the narratives to make Guests feel as though *they* were the stars of the show playing the roles of the lead characters. Snow White's Adventures followed the fairest one of all's escape from the Queen's castle to the Seven Dwarfs' cottage, focusing primarily on her nightmarish journey through the Dark Forest. Peter Pan Flight traced the Darling children's moonlit flight from their nursery to Never Land. And Mr. Toad's Wild Ride gave Guests the chance to get

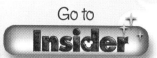
THESE PAGES: Four of Walt Disney's animated classics—*Snow White and the Seven Dwarfs, Alice in Wonderland, Peter Pan,* and the "Wind in the Willows" segment of *The Adventures of Ichabod and Mr. Toad,* all destined to become beloved attractions in Fantasyland at Disneyland.

OPPOSITE, MIDDLE: Two young Disneyland Guests discover "motor mania" in a Mr. Toad "motorcar."

OPPOSITE, BOTTOM: Walt Disney casts a careful eye on one of Peter Pan Flight's flying pirate galleons. When a new attraction was ready to test, Walt was always the first to ride.

behind the wheel of a "motorcar," the latest object of Toad's mania, and follow their amphibian hero on a reckless trek across the English countryside.

Further strengthening the cinematic influence on the Park, Walt recruited longtime animation background artist Claude Coats to work his environmental magic on the Fantasyland dark rides. "At that time," Claude said, "most of the black light rides were little scare rides where a skeleton rattled and a skull popped out. But Ken's storyboards showed that Mr. Toad or Peter Pan or Snow White could be told, not quite as a story, but at least as a mood that gave you the feeling of that story."

It was another inspired casting decision on Walt's part. Just as Claude had made an inspired use of color in the backgrounds of the animated features, he brought the same striking sense of mood and emotion to the attractions that transformed those same films into three-dimensional reality. Claude's palette of eye-popping fluorescent colors in the Fantasyland attractions elevated them well beyond the amusement park spook rides and fun houses of the past.

The dark rides were built at the Walt Disney Studios. Mock-ups of the attractions were laid out in a sweat-inducing tin-roofed shed, enabling the Imagineers to visualize spatial relationships and experience the show from a guest's point of view. Dark-ride vehicles traditionally had steel wheels, but they were far too noisy for the attractions Walt envisioned. "We're trying to tell a story in those rides; we need quiet cars." To that end, he hired the Arrow Development Company to design new ride vehicles that were much quieter and more maneuverable than their "amusement pier" predecessors.

Walt dropped in on his Imagineers every day to monitor their progress on the dark rides. Peter Pan Flight was his favorite, and with good reason. Like so many other Walt Disney productions before it, the attraction was a first—a fly-through ride with pirate ship vehicles suspended from the ceiling. As the Park's opening day drew closer, Walt himself rode them again and again in marathon sessions. The Imagineers quickly learned to recognize their boss's reaction. If Walt was happy, he hopped out of his pirate ship or mine car with a wink and a smile. If the experience wasn't up to his exacting standards, the infamous Disney eyebrow shot up, and he barked, "Fix this thing and let's get this show on the road."

The dark rides quickly proved to be among the most popular attractions in the Park. "When we were planning Fantasyland," Walt once said, "I recalled the lyrics of the song, 'When You Wish Upon a Star.' The words of that melody inspired us to create a land where dreams could actually come true." And where the Disney animated classics come to life and immerse the audience in worlds of wonder previously confined to the animated films. At long last, people could come to Hollywood and really *see* something.

THIS PAGE: The exquisitely detailed Fantasyland attraction buildings for (clockwise from top) Pinocchio's Daring Journey, Mr. Toad's Wild Ride, Snow White's Scary Adventures, Alice in Wonderland, and Peter Pan's Flight.

A New Fantasyland Fulfills an Old Dream

The dark rides quickly proved to be among the most popular attractions in Disneyland. Guests did indeed jump at the chance to "live" some of the most memorable moments from their favorite animated features. But at the same, time, it became clear that they'd rather *see* their favorite characters than *be* them. In fact, in an August 12, 1955, memo, Fantasyland manager George Whitney noted that Guests were "confused at not seeing Snow White, Peter Pan, or Mr. Toad." The Imagineers had always intended the audience itself to be the star of these three-dimensional "living movies," effectively taking the place of the films' heroes. "Since it is almost impossible to convey this thought properly to the people," George continued, "it might be best to put an animated Peter Pan or appropriate character in these rides." As it turned out, it would be more than thirty years before the Imagineers solved this particular conceptual problem once and for all.

In the early 1980s, the Imagineers were given a green light to completely redesign Fantasyland and update the dark rides in particular so they could keep pace with newer, more thrilling attractions such as Space Mountain and Big Thunder Mountain Railroad. Veteran Imagineers, such as Rolly Crump and Ken Anderson, joined creative forces with newer recruits, such as designer Tony Baxter and architect Brock Thoman, to create a new Fantasyland that was more in line with Walt's original vision.

Gone were the land's cost-effective festival facades and tournament tents, replaced by facsimiles of Toad Hall, old London Town, and the Queen's castle. Almost thirty years after Disneyland's opening day, Fantasyland was finally the whimsical storybook village of Walt's dreams. The attractions themselves now boasted state-of-the-art special effects, and, for the first time in Fantasyland, Audio-Animatronics figures. The three original dark rides were joined by an all-new animated adventure, Pinocchio's Daring Journey, with a new and improved Alice in Wonderland attraction following in 1984.

The Imagineers also took advantage of the opportunity to finally eliminate the confusion that resulted from the original creative team's decision to let Guests fill in for the lead characters. And so Snow White herself finally got a role in the attraction that bears her name, Snow White's Adventures, which in the process became Snow White's Scary Adventures, a veritable rite of passage for younger Disneyland Guests thanks to the ubiquitous Witch. Pinocchio, Peter Pan, and Alice also put in frequent appearances in their respective attractions, although, curiously enough, Mr. Toad is depicted only as a stone statue, twice at Toad Hall and once again in a village square.

The New Fantasyland officially opened on May 23, 1983, with Alice in Wonderland premiering in April 1984, finally living up to Walt Disney's early description of a visit to Fantasyland. "What youngster hasn't dreamed of flying with Peter Pan over moonlit London?" he asked. "Here in the 'happiest kingdom of them all,' you can journey with Snow White through the dark forest to the diamond mine of the Seven Dwarfs, flee the clutches of Mr. Smee and Captain Hook with Peter Pan, and race with Mr. Toad in his wild auto ride through the streets of old London Town. The time you spend in this carefree kingdom will be a dream come true—for everyone who is young at heart."

Walt Disney Imagineering

The Gold Standard:
Fifty Years of Show Quality
at
Disneyland

by Dave Fisher

The good news is that Disneyland, the first Disney park and a treasured international icon of fantasy and imagination, has been celebrating its golden anniversary this year in dazzling style and with stunning spectacle, from the bejeweled Sleeping Beauty Castle and the "reimagined" Space Mountain, to an all-new parade and a nighttime music, lights, and fireworks spectacular.

The better news is that the Park, even at fifty years old, is still perhaps the fairest of them all, looking just as fresh, clean, and charming today as it did when it opened on July 17, 1955—maybe even more so.

And that's no small, easy—or even magical—feat.

Let's face it. By the time we reach the half-century mark, we've probably all seen better days. Though we may still feel young, we may not look so young anymore, tempting some of us to do a little nip here, a bit of a tuck there.

Normally, a facelift would lead to much twittering and nattering, not all of it positive (okay, very little of it positive). But in the case of Disneyland, its "refreshment" has been met with wholesale praise, to put it modestly. (*If* the Park was to brag just a little, it would say that the response has been overwhelming, with Disneyland Guest Relations being inundated with thousands of upbeat comments about how great Disneyland looks for a fifty-year-old.)

However, though Disneyland did receive a somewhat noticeable makeover in the year leading up to the celebration, it wasn't anything out of the ordinary. In fact, over the last fifty years, Disneyland has been receiving "a little nip here, a bit of a tuck there" on almost an annual basis. And "The Happiest Place on Earth" is not alone. Every Disney park around the world is always undergoing some kind of freshening or rejuvenation beyond the addition of new lands, attractions, shops, and restaurants.

It can be something as simple as a new coat of paint on a building, such as Main Street, U.S.A.'s Emporium, or as complex as a complete audio, lighting, and controls hardware and software upgrade to a venerable attraction, such as Walt Disney's Enchanted Tiki Room. In some cases, a familiar attraction may be "enhanced" with new show scenes, as was the case with the Jungle Cruise at Disneyland, which now features attacking piranhas and a rather explosive situation for the apes who have commandeered the explorer camp.

Although the upkeep is a team effort on the part of the maintenance, facilities, and operations teams at each of the Disney parks, a small group of Imagineers with the rather staid name of Show Quality Standards (SQS, for short) plays a key local and global role in making sure a park such as Disneyland and all its attractions, shops, restaurants, walkways, waterfalls, wall and floor coverings, landscaping, railings, colors, signs, and everything else remain true to their initial design.

OPPOSITE PAGE: "Before and After" pictures showing examples of the loving care applied to Sleeping Beauty Castle, Main Street, U.S.A., and the shopping bazaar in Adventureland.

"We partner with the parks and resorts to help solve problems and maintain the original creative intent," says George Head, vice president of Walt Disney Imagineering Global SQS. "Our Guests notice the difference as much as we do, and we always feel it's better to handle things as they come rather than let them build up to a point where it seriously starts to impact the Guest experience."

During Disneyland's first decade, SQS didn't exist, and there was a reason for that.

"In the early years, Walt Disney performed the function," says Head, who was the first Show Quality Standards liaison at Tokyo Disneyland in 1983 and has been involved with SQS operations ever since. "He used to walk the Park almost every Saturday morning, and you can bet that his notes were probably taken care of by Monday."

The Show Quality Standards organization itself came into being with the opening of Epcot in 1982. With three parks to maintain now (Disneyland and Magic Kingdom Park at Walt Disney World were the other two) and a fourth (Tokyo Disneyland) on the way within the year, Imagineer Wathel Rogers was given the task of assembling and managing the group of Imagineers who would support the teams operating the parks. After all, if anyone knew what Walt Disney was looking for on his weekly walks through Disneyland, it was Rogers. Originally a machinist in the Studio crafts shop, Rogers had helped build the miniature scale railroad that steamed around Walt Disney's home. He was also instrumental in the development of Audio-Animatronics technology, which brought lifelike movements to mechanical, three-dimensional birds, flowers, bears, pirates, and even a version of Abraham Lincoln.

And Rogers knew that if there was anyone who understood anything about the history and design of Disney parks, it was the artists, writers, technicians, designers, and managers at Walt Disney Imagineering. Known at the time as WED (for Walter Elias Disney) Enterprises, Imagineering had been formed in 1952 by Walt Disney himself to plan, design, and build Disneyland. The first Imagineers were picked from the Walt Disney Studios' best creative talent. Today, a new generation of Imagineers, representing more than 140 different disciplines, has ably assumed the mantle of developing Disney parks, resorts, cruise ships, and attractions, as well as maintaining the "creative integrity" of those Disney entertainment kingdoms in the years after they've welcomed their first guests.

Worldwide, just over 50 of Walt Disney Imagineering's 1,400 Imagineers have been assigned to Show Quality Standards, troubleshooting technical issues, helping Park Cast Members in operations and maintenance understand what Imagineers call "show awareness" (that is, the underlying stories and reasons things were designed the way they were), and identifying, documenting, and rectifying those areas that need attention. (Another fifty Imagineers are part of Design

Services teams at each resort, which handle new work, as well as additions and enhancements to existing facilities.)

The dedication of that small core of illustrators, graphic artists, animation programmers, lighting designers, audio engineers, special effects technicians, color stylists, figure finishers, documentation experts, rockwork specialists, and other craftsmen, coordinators, and planners to the SQS effort is legendary, even among their fellow Imagineers.

Take the team that staffs the Disneyland Resort SQS office in Anaheim, California. Back in 2002, when Disneyland was a mere forty-seven years old, director of Disneyland Resort SQS Stan Dodd and show designer Tom LaDuke made an assessment of what they believed needed to be accomplished at the Park prior to its fiftieth anniversary. Though scrupulously maintained over the years, Disneyland had become a little rough around the edges, which is to be expected of anyone or anything heading toward the half-century mark.

"Sometimes, it's easy to let the little things go because you're so focused on the big picture," says Dodd, "the new attractions, the new lands, the new parks. What we wanted to do was get everyone to concentrate on the details. Our goal was and always has been to address those areas that need it before the problem gets too big. It was a pretty big list."

After nearly two years of analysis, evaluation, and preparation, the SQS team was given the go-ahead—with a little less than a year to do the work.

"We're not just talking about a coat of paint here," says Dodd. "Some things were almost completely rebuilt."

What made the "Sparkle" program (as it came to be called) so challenging was not so much the amount of time the team had to do the projects (though that was important), but the fact that Disneyland is open every day. That meant the work had to be done mostly in the dead of night. Any work done during the day had to have as little effect on the guest experience as possible. Compromises were negotiated: some buildings, including Sleeping Beauty Castle and facades on Main Street, were wrapped in scaffolding and tarps for extended periods of time, but the noisy and intrusive work, such as hammering, sawing, and the use of heavy machinery, was reserved for the night shift.

The most noticeable differences were to the exterior facades of buildings in Tomorrowland, on Main Street, and in

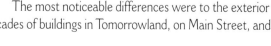

New Orleans Square. City Hall was rebuilt almost from the ground up, extensive repairs were made to the fronts of the shops that line Front and Royal Streets in Disneyland's re-creation of the Crescent City, and Space Mountain was returned to its classic white.

Individual attractions were also "refreshed." The SQS and Design Services teams combined forces to overhaul Walt Disney's Enchanted Tiki Room, installing new lighting, audio and controls systems, rebuilding the pre-show area, and replacing the thatch roof. The Jungle Cruise was extensively re-landscaped, new show scenes were added, the lighting was enhanced for after-dark excursions, and the skipper's spiels were revamped (and here you thought they were just ad-libbing all this time). The Haunted Mansion received an overall cleanup and new effects, including an updated series of changing portraits in the gallery guests walk through prior to the boarding the "doom buggies" and a "floating head" effect in the séance room.

"It takes extremely passionate, committed, self-sacrificing individuals to devote this much time and effort to sweating the details," says Dodd. "We at SQS see ourselves as the Jiminy Cricket of the parks, the creative conscience that reminds everyone in our organization that our Guests do appreciate what we do, even if they can't quite put their finger on what exactly has been done."

Now that Disneyland seems shinier, newer, and more colorful in celebration of its fiftieth anniversary, one would think the SQS team is ready for a breather, but that's far from the case. After all, the Park is almost fifty-one years old—and the Walt Disney Imagineering SQS team is determined to keep it looking the same today as it was the day Walt Disney welcomed everyone who came to this "happy place."

But they're going to have to do it without Stan Dodd. He moved on to Hong Kong Disneyland, where he assembled and is overseeing a new Show Quality Standards team. Even in the newest of the Disney parks, it's never too early to get started on the sparkle. ✪

THIS PAGE: Exquisite richness and fine attention to detail abound in City Hall on Main Street, U.S.A., at Triton's Gardens in Fantasyland, and at the Enchanted Tiki Room in Adventureland—all freshly decked out for the 50th Anniversary celebration.

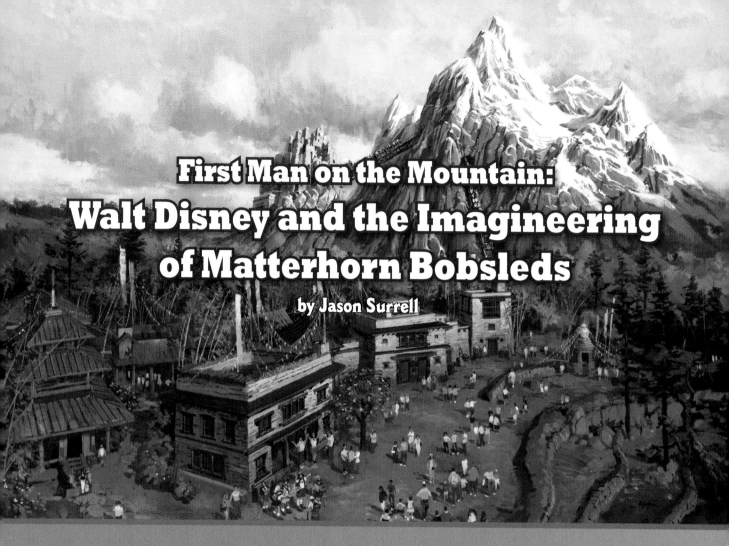

First Man on the Mountain:
Walt Disney and the Imagineering of Matterhorn Bobsleds

by Jason Surrell

I f you're looking for a challenge, there's a good chance you'll find one on a mountain somewhere in the world. Mountains are what separate the men from the boys, figuratively speaking. They've long possessed symbolic value in both human culture and the story arts. Mountains represent adversity, exploration and discovery. They've also come to stand for change, and they mark significant rites of passage, often figuring into the journey from childhood into the adult world. And in the vast and diverse world of story—from cave paintings and campfire tales to pulp fiction and blockbuster movies—they often serve as central locations for the most pivotal plot points. Whether it's Mount Sinai, Mount Olympus, Mount Doom, or Mount Rushmore, significant story events can be counted on to take place on or around a mountaintop.

It should come as no surprise then, that some of the most compelling, memorable, and enduring attractions at the Disney theme parks are set on, around, and inside mountains, providing dramatic backdrops for the most fantastic adventures. The Disney mountains, too, often serve as rites of passage for younger guests, who count down the days to that fateful Disneyland trip when they will finally be tall enough—and brave enough—to take on Space Mountain. Or Big Thunder Mountain. Or Splash Mountain. With so many

such "challenges" to choose from, it's clear that Walt and his Imagineers learned long ago that mountain settings could be just as effective in the three-dimensional storytelling world of the Disney theme parks as they are on the printed page or the big screen.

This year, Walt Disney World carries on the tradition with the opening of Expedition Everest: Legend of the Forbidden Mountain at Disney's Animal Kingdom Park. The Disney mountain has played a leading role in the themed show for over forty-five years, and the debut of Mount Everest is a fitting occasion to look back at the "E"-Ticket adventure that started it all: Matterhorn Bobsleds at Disneyland.

One of the Park's most beloved attractions exists because Walt Disney literally made a mountain out of a molehill. The concept originated one day in late 1956, when Walt and Disneyland construction chief Joe Fowler were sitting atop Holiday Hill, a wooded knoll in the middle of the Park that separated Fantasyland from Tomorrowland. It took its name from Walt's early plans for Holidayland, a seasonal special events area that was earmarked for the site but was never built at that location.

The "hill" was originally just a twenty-foot pile of dirt created when the construction crew dug the nearby Sleeping Beauty Castle moat. To make it appear as though the mound

THESE PAGES: Expedition Everest: Legend of the Forbidden Mountain at Disney's Animal Kingdom (*opposite*) is the latest addition to the Disney mountain ranges, which include the thrills of Space Mountain, Big Thunder Mountain Railroad, Splash Mountain—and of course, Matterhorn Mountain, found only at Disneyland.

61

was supposed to be there, the enterprising crew leveled off the top, laid down some sod, and added some park benches and trees, creating a makeshift picnic area they playfully dubbed "Lookout Mountain." Despite their best aesthetic efforts, the hill was an eyesore for Imagineers and a challenge for the Disneyland operations team in that it had become something of a "lover's lane" for more daring Park guests. Compounding the problem, Holiday Hill was also home to an unsightly steel tower that supported the cable for the Park's Skyway ride.

"You know, Joe," Walt said to Joe as they sat atop the hill, "why don't we make some snow and have a toboggan ride here?" The construction veteran explained that it would be hard to maintain the snow, especially in the sweltering California summers, and that water drainage would be a challenge due to inevitable—and constant—thawing. Once Walt got excited about an idea, however, it was hard to get him to let go of it, and, as usual, his enthusiasm quickly won over everyone else. The Park's operators even went so far as to rename their mini-mountain "Snow Hill" in the hope that Walt would one day get his toboggan ride.

Meanwhile, Disneyland executive Jack Sayers read a *Funspot* magazine article about wild mouse–style roller coasters and sent it to Walt, suggesting that such a ride on Snow Hill—with some artificial snow completing the illusion—might be a more practical alternative than an actual toboggan run. Walt, in turn, passed it along to the Imagineers at WED, where the concept was given further consideration.

By the end of 1957, Walt had made the decision to bulldoze Snow Hill altogether and build a man-made attraction, whose name was upgraded to the more impressive-sounding Snow Mountain, in its place. During a 1958 meeting

with Walt, Imagineer Bill Cottrell described a ride that was to consist of "a pair of wild-mouse bobsleds on Snow Hill." In fact, the 1958 Disneyland Souvenir Map actually depicts a Snow Mountain, with the Skyway's steel support structure protruding from its peak. Additional names considered during the period included Mount Disneyland, Disneyland Mountain, Sorcerer's Mountain, Magic Mountain (which would go on to find fame elsewhere), Fantasy Mountain, and Echo Mountain. The Imagineering team even playfully suggests a Swiss variation on the boss's own name: the Valterhorn.

They were getting closer with that last suggestion. The Disney family often vacationed in Europe, and Walt had developed an affinity for the scenic beauty and storybook architecture of Switzerland in particular. In 1956, he had even built a Swiss chalet–style station for the Skyway in Fantasyland. As the Imagineers continued to play with ideas for Snow Mountain, Walt spent some time in the Swiss Alps during the 1958 filming of *Third Man on the Mountain*, a coming-of-age adventure starring Michael Rennie, James MacArthur, and Janet Munro.

The grace and majesty of the distinctively shaped, snow-capped Matterhorn positively captivated Walt. He immediately sent his Imagineers a postcard of the Matterhorn with two simple words scrawled across the back: "Build this!" That made it official: the Imagineering team was to create a scale replica of the Matterhorn with wild mouse–style bobsleds racing down and around it. In January 1958, the attraction officially became known as Matterhorn Mountain.

With their marching orders clearly written on that fateful postcard, the Imagineers put on their sorcerer hats and went to work. Vic Green became the project's art director, Joe Fowler took his usual place in charge of construction and WED's resident transportation wizard, Bob Gurr, worked on the design of the bobsled ride—or roller coaster—itself. "Designing the bobsled track plan was probably the hardest project I ever worked on," Bob told *The "E" Ticket* magazine. "I had failed geometry in high school and had to teach myself trigonometry to design the track."

Since the usual two-dimensional drawings and blueprints would prove to be hopelessly inadequate to build such

OPPOSITE: One of Walt's most popular contract players, James MacArthur, starred with acclaimed character actor Michael Rennie in *Third Man on the Mountain* (1959), but the film's real star was the mighty Matterhorn, called the Citadel in the movie.

BELOW CENTER, LEFT AND RIGHT: During a visit to Switzerland, Walt fell in love with the charms of the Matterhorn. Less than a year after location filming wrapped in Switzerland in January 1959, Walt was presenting his own version of the Matterhorn at Disneyland.

BOTTOM: The famous (or is it infamous?) predecessor of Disneyland Park's Matterhorn, Holiday Hill. Today, the Matterhorn proudly stands on the site of this dirt pile, which for the first few years served as a "hideaway" for amorous Disneyland guests.

ABOVE: At 147 feet high and about 1/100th the size of the real deal in Switzerland, Matterhorn Mountain at Disneyland is home to the Matterhorn Bobsleds, the first steel-tracked roller coaster and the first with multiple cars on the track at the same time—revolutionizing the roller-coaster industry.

BELOW: Walt and Admiral Joe Fowler take a thrilling first test run on the uncompleted bobsled attraction.

BACKGROUND: Daring mountain climbers can sometimes be spotted ascending the icy peak of Disneyland's Matterhorn Mountain.

OPPOSITE: Though the Matterhorn Bobsleds was the first roller coaster–like attraction at Disneyland, it was not the first considered: as seen in this test run, Casey Jr. from Walt Disney's *Dumbo* was originally intended to be so honored, but the attraction never made it past the testing stages.

a unique and oddly-shaped structure, Fred Joerger and the WED Model Shop built a number of three-dimensional models of the mountain so everyone could see what the Matterhorn looked like from every perspective. It seems to have worked: the last in this line of models bears an uncanny resemblance to the Matterhorn as it was ultimately built.

Walt's bobsled ride may have presented a series of seemingly insurmountable construction and engineering challenges, but the Imagineers weren't in it alone. Walt also recruited Ed Morgan and Karl Bacon of the engineering firm Arrow Development Company to help design a new kind of roller coaster inside his mountain. Arrow was no stranger to Walt's unconventional and often, at first glance, impossible requests. The firm had developed the ride systems for many of Disneyland's early attractions, including Mr. Toad's Wild Ride and the Casey Jr. Circus Train, but they had never designed a roller coaster. That worked out well for everyone, considering that the Matterhorn was shaping up to be anything but a typical amusement park "scream machine."

Arrow collaborated with WED and came up with a ride system that would forever change roller coasters and revolutionize the amusement industry. The system consisted of two separate rides that would weave in and out of each other's path as they snaked down and around a faux Matterhorn with the existing Skyway running straight through the middle of the mountain. Perhaps most revolutionary was their use of tubular steel pipe rails instead of the traditional flat rails. The cars "connected" to the track in three different places and the wheels "hugged" the tubes in a way that restricted vertical

movement of the car, creating a much safer and smoother ride than the traditional wooden coaster. The new system also allowed the track to twist and turn beyond any roller coaster before it, all the better to simulate the sudden dips and hairpin turns of an authentic bobsled ride.

In early 1959, WED and Arrow were joined by American Bridge, the firm charged with constructing the steel endoskeleton of the Matterhorn. The mountain's gargantuan framework rose from the bulldozed Snow Hill, encasing (and thus hiding) the unsightly Skyway tower; the cars would now pass straight through the Matterhorn on their way to and from the Fantasyland and Tomorrowland stations.

With the mountain's steel skeleton in place, the construction team added a layer of plywood that would both shape and support the faux rockwork to come. Hundreds of wooden forms of all shapes and sizes were cut out and put together like a giant, three-dimensional puzzle to give the Matterhorn its distinctive profile. The crew then applied the rockwork itself from the top of the mountain down, burying the plywood beneath tons of concrete that were intricately sculpted to form the alpine slopes, icy caverns, and towering waterfalls of the majestic Matterhorn.

The bobsled ride is considered the world's first "steel coaster," a vast improvement over the teeth-rattling, headache-inducing wooden coasters of the past. Arrow's innovative new Ride Control System also made the Matterhorn the first coaster to allow multiple cars to run on one track at the same time, which doubtless came as a great relief to the Disneyland operations team.

Walt had his mountain; now all he needed was a bobsled ride to go with it. Sandbags took the earliest test rides. The first human subject was Bob Gurr, who was recruited for the job by machine-shop supervisor Roger Broggie with the none-too-reassuring observation: "You designed the track, now you can be the first to ride it."

Soon, Vic Green, Joe Fowler, and Walt himself were all going for rides. Walt was particularly eager to take the new bobsleds for a test spin down the slopes of his mountain. The only problem was that the ride wasn't finished and the track ran out somewhere near the end of the run, a nightmare common among coaster-phobics. Undaunted, Walt had Joe Fowler place a huge pile of hay at the end of the track for a softer landing. After several successful such "hay rides," Walt turned to Joe and exclaimed, "Hey, this is great! Can't we find some way to add all this hay to the show?" An alpine lake made for a more aesthetically pleasing and thematically appropriate substitute.

Walt's Matterhorn was exactly one one-hundredth the height of the real deal, 147 feet versus 14,700 feet. The mountain was composed of 2,175 individual steel girders—none the same length as another—multiple tons of cement, and enough lumber to build 27 tract homes. The attraction was completed at a final cost of $1.5 million, an expensive addition even by 1959 standards.

Matterhorn Bobsleds opened on June 14, 1959, along with Submarine Voyage and the Disneyland-Alweg Monorail System, with a live, ninety-minute television broadcast. With so many attractions premiering at once, the day was considered nothing less than "the second opening of Disneyland." In fact, the three new additions were so elaborate (and expensive!) that Guests had to purchase a higher priced ticket, the "E," in order to experience them. The "E" Ticket joined the existing "A," "B," "C," and "D" denominations, and was reserved exclusively for the Park's top attractions. That gives Matterhorn Bobsleds the distinction of being one of the very first "E" Ticket adventures, ushering in a bold new era of Disneyland attractions.

Matterhorn Bobsleds was an instant hit with guests and quickly became one of the Park's most popular attractions, a distinction it still enjoys over forty-five years later. That's not to say that the Imagineers didn't wave their wands now and again to help the groundbreaking attraction keep its edge. The most elaborate enhancement took place in June 1978, when the Imagineering team focused as much attention on the mountain's insides as they had on the outside in 1959.

Until that time, much of the Matterhorn's interior was scenically unfinished, and portions of the steel support structure were clearly visible to riders. In June 1978, the attraction saw the addition of sparkling ice caverns, a special effects "snowstorm," tandem bobsleds that effectively doubled the ride's capacity, and a "mysterious, lurking snow monster" (as the Imagineers described it)—better known as the Abominable Snowman. The new show elements were promoted with the cryptic question: "What's gotten into the Matterhorn?" and the ominous image of a pair of glaring red eyes.

There have been a number of other changes since the Abominable Snowman began prowling the mountain in 1978. The Skyway sent its last car gliding through the Matterhorn in 1994. Imagineers added the "lost Wells Expedition" to the ice cavern scene a year later as a tribute to the late Frank Wells, an avid mountain climber and The Walt Disney Company's President and Chief Operating Officer from 1984 until he was killed in a helicopter crash in 1994.

Shortly before Matterhorn Bobsleds opened in 1959, Joe Fowler turned to Walt Disney and said of the mammoth and literally and figuratively groundbreaking construction project: "I think we'll have it finished on time, but next time, when we have to build a mountain, let's let God do it."

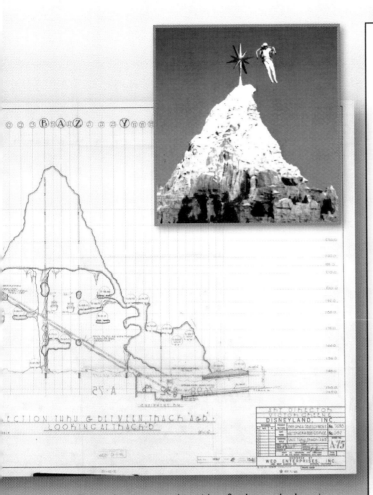

As told in tales of old, way up high in the Himalayan mountains...

...there lives a fierce and mysterious creature that protects these faraway lands. Passersby on foot or rail had better beware, for so seldom the few, if any, live to tell the frightening tale of the forbidden mountain and what stands guard over its domain. Locals know this mysterious creature as the Yeti, but it is more commonly known as the Abominable Snowman. He has protected these mountain lands since the beginning of time, and the locals revere him as much as they fear him.

This year, at Disney's Animal Kingdom Theme Park at the Walt Disney World Resort, guests will have their chance to explore this mysterious realm and try to catch a fleeting glimpse of the guardian of the mountain. If they're lucky, they'll return to tell the tale. The journey begins at Expedition Everest, on an old thirty-four-passenger train at the foot of the Everest mountain range in a local Himalayan village right in the middle of the Yeti's land. Once these brave explorers embark, they ascend to the snowcapped peaks but beware—danger is around every bend and the journey becomes a white-knuckle, hair-raising adventure full of fun. Guests travel over rickety bridges and glide down icy glacial slopes. *Wait! Was that the Yeti? The track! It's gone! Oh no! We're sliding down backwards! What's that in the shadows?* For those who want to find out and who are brave enough to test their physical and emotional well being, get ready for the adventure of a lifetime! Expedition Everest-Legend of the Forbidden Mountain will be an unforgettable journey full of mystery, wonder, and surprise!

What does it take to bring this mysterious creature to life? Disney sent a team of researchers on an expedition to the Himalayan lands to study the local lore of the Yeti and the way of life of the people of Nepal and China. They brought back sketches, artifacts, photographs, documented Yeti sightings, and a story rich in local lore and customs that they planned to retell in Florida. To do this, the Imagineers built Florida's highest mountain peak, coming in just under 200 feet (the real Everest stands at 29,035 feet). The overall design was inspired by the Wasatch Mountains and Imagineer Joe Rohde's photos of his personal expeditions to the Himalayas. The village building design utilized a technique called "rammed earth" in which slightly moistened dirt is hammered with mallets until it acquires the consistency of adobe. Properly protected, the buildings could last for a thousand years. There are over 2,000 handcrafted items from Asia in the architectural ornamentation, 1,800 tons of steel in the mountain (six times the amount of an office building of similar height), and 128 species of plants and shrubs, including Giant Bamboo. The entire Everest mountain range, Disney Everest that is, sits on over six acres in the land of Asia in Disney's Animal Kingdom Theme Park.

Go to

Insider

www.Disney.com/DisneyInsider

by Jeff Titelius

But such was not to be, either for Joe or the Imagineers who would follow him in the decades to come. The Matterhorn proved to be just as compelling a setting for a theme park story as so many other peaks had been for us over the centuries, in life and in art. And, just as the mountain has provided life-changing experiences for everyone from the primitive tribesman of the distant past to the modern day thrill-seeker, the Matterhorn—and all the Disney mountains—continues to serve as a true rite of passage for millions of kids who want their parents to recognize that they've grown up. With the Matterhorn, "the mountain" had come to Walt, and it would prove to be only the first of many iconic landmarks that would one day come to make up Disney's "E" Ticket range.

TOP: During the 1965 Christmas season, the amazing "Rocket Man," William P. Suitor, soared out of Tomorrowland and over the Matterhorn, powered by his futuristic Rocket Belt. Though the Rocket Man is a well-remembered, well-celebrated Disneyland image, he only flew for those few weeks in 1965.

ABOVE: An original WED Enterprises blueprint for the Matterhorn, showing the "up-ramp" through the center of the mountain.

OPPOSITE: Original promotional art for the Matterhorn, artist unknown.

The Sun Never Sets on a Disney Park

by Dave Fisher

*I*n fall 2001, a group of Walt Disney Imagineers stood on the exact spot where just four years later guests would be posing for photos in front of Sleeping Beauty Castle at Hong Kong Disneyland. It's a good thing no one rocked the boat because if that had happened, that would have literally been one wet group of Imagineers.

You see, back in 2001, the place where Sleeping Beauty Castle—and, for that matter, where all of Hong Kong Disneyland Resort is today— was Penny's Bay, an inlet on the northeast end of Lantau Island in Hong Kong.

After transforming orange groves in Anaheim, California, into "The Happiest Place on Earth," swamps and cow pastures in central Florida into the "Vacation Kingdom of the World," a flat landfill next to Tokyo Bay into the "Kingdom of Family Dreams" and rolling farmland outside Paris into an enchanted realm with a Château de La Belle au Bois Dormant, Imagineers faced perhaps the greatest challenge of their more than fifty years of planning, designing, and building Disney parks and resorts: turning water into land.

Okay, so they had a little help from the Hong Kong government, which took responsibility for reclaiming Penny's Bay and providing Imagineers with 500 acres of land on which to build hotels, castles, mountains, and a landing pad for elephants that fly. The government also handled the building of streets, walkways, bridges, and utilities, as well as a manmade lake, an arboretum, and a ferry pier. (Walt Disney Imagineering did lend its expertise to the design of the government facilities, which also included police and fire stations and a special rail line to the resort constructed by the MTR Corporation, the operator of Hong Kong's ultramodern Mass Transit Railway system, or MTR, for short.)

Though Hong Kong Disneyland is magical now, there was certainly nothing magical about the hard work it took to make it that way. Turning Penny's Bay into Hong Kong Disneyland was a complex and difficult undertaking, but it was a feat accomplished with remarkable efficiency.

The project was announced on November 1, 1999, and an official agreement between the Hong Kong Special Administrative Region (SAR) government and The Walt Disney Company was signed a little over a month later, on December 10. Reclamation of Penny's Bay began in the summer of 2000 and was completed two years later. After a ground-breaking ceremony was held on the site on January 12, 2003, the project immediately kicked into high gear. Originally scheduled to open in late 2005 or early 2006, the opening date was pushed forward to September 12, 2005, as contractors and Imagineers

made faster-than-anticipated progress.

The grand opening of Hong Kong Disneyland was a *watershed* event in a milestone year for Disney parks and resorts. On May 5, 2005, Disney kicked off the "Happiest Celebration on Earth," a worldwide event saluting the fiftieth anniversary of Disneyland and celebrated at Disney destinations around the globe.

The event, marked the largest debut of Disney park attractions and entertainment ever. At Disneyland, "The Happiest Celebration on Earth" became the "Happiest Homecoming on Earth" as "The Happiest Place on Earth" (okay, enough already) welcomed a new parade (Walt Disney's Parade of Dreams), a new fireworks spectacular (Remember…Dreams Come True), a new attraction (Buzz Lightyear Astro Blasters), the return of a "re-Imagineered" classic attraction (Space Mountain), a tribute to the first fifty years of Disneyland with a film starring Steve Martin and Donald Duck, and a Sleeping Beauty Castle decked out with "crown" jewels and gold finery.

ABOVE: An unusual mountain background for Sleeping Beauty Castle—not the Matterhorn! This castle was patterned after the original Sleeping Beauty Castle at Disneyland, marking the first time that design has been re-created.

OPPOSITE, TOP: Cast members assemble for their first group photo.

OPPOSITE, MIDDLE: An aerial view of the Hong Kong Disneyland Resort during final construction.

OPPOSITE, BOTTOM: Anxious crowds wait to enter the Park in this view taken from Main Street Station.

Walt Disney World Resort in Florida joined the festivities by "importing" attractions and shows from other Disney parks around the world: Magic Kingdom Park added "Cinderellabration," a musical direct from Tokyo Disneyland; Epcot debuted the popular Soarin' hang-gliding adventure from Disney's California Adventure; Disney Studios revved up its act with the Lights, Motors, Action! Extreme Stunt Show from Walt Disney Studios in France; and Disney's Animal Kingdom Park featured a limited engagement of Lucky the Dinosaur, the first free-roaming Audio-Animatronics figure, who was borrowed from the R&D labs at Walt Disney Imagineering. (After his stint there, Lucky obtained his passport, packed his bags, and headed for Hong Kong Disneyland, where he spent the fall of 2005.)

The celebration wasn't limited to the United States. Disneyland Resort Paris launched its own "re-Imagineered" Space Mountain, called Space Mountain: Mission 2, and added a new nighttime fireworks show called Wishes.

On the other side of the world, Tokyo Disneyland joined in with a tribute to the 1950s (when both Disneyland and rock 'n roll were born) dubbed "Rock Around the Mouse." And Tokyo DisneySea featured the opening of Raging Spirits, a high-speed adventure that's the first attraction at the Tokyo Disney Resort to boast a vertical 360° loop.

Hong Kong Disneyland became part of "The Happiest Celebration on Earth" with its grand opening on September 12, 2005. Like all of the Disney parks that have come before it, Hong Kong Disneyland offers a full day of family entertainment in a magical kingdom of dreams, imagination, wonder, and adventure. It also has a few unique things of its own.

Perhaps the most striking is its location. The park is surrounded by verdant hills that provide a stunning backdrop not found in any other Disney park around the world. The hotels have it double, with the hills and the park on one side and expansive views of the South China Sea and, on clear days, Hong Kong Island on the other.

"What I like best about Hong Kong Disneyland is the location," says John Verity, managing director of the Hong Kong Disneyland resort for Walt Disney Imagineering, echoing the words of just about every Imagineer who worked on the project. "I think that the location is just spectacular. Located between two hills, this is the most unique Disney park that's ever been done anywhere."

Another notable aspect of the Park is its uncanny resemblance to Disneyland in California. Although Magic Kingdom Park in Florida, Tokyo Disneyland in Japan, and Disneyland Paris in France follow the general layout of the original Disneyland, Hong Kong Disneyland is the first of the Magic Kingdom–style parks to actually be based on that first park, right down to the scope and scale of Main Street, U.S.A., and the presence of Sleeping Beauty Castle, an almost exact duplicate of the one in Anaheim. In fact, in size and number of attractions at opening,

Hong Kong Disneyland is remarkably like Disneyland in 1955.

"We designed Hong Kong Disneyland to showcase some of the best attractions and elements from other Disney parks," says Tom Morris, who was Imagineering's lead designer on the project, "but Hong Kong Disneyland is its own park. While it may be very much like Disneyland, it is also very different."

That becomes readily apparent the moment visitors pass beneath the railroad tracks just inside the main entrance and see a familiar plaque that reads "Here you leave today and enter the world of yesterday, tomorrow, and fantasy"—but here it is in two languages.

Actually, Hong Kong Disneyland often uses three languages: English, a nod to the fact that this is an American park in Hong Kong (and that many people in Hong Kong still speak English, owing to the fact it was once a British possession); Cantonese, the language spoken by most people who live in Hong Kong; and Putonghua, the official language of mainland China.

As if that weren't confusing enough, there are also two written languages in China: traditional Chinese characters (primarily used in Hong Kong and Taiwan) and simplified Chinese characters (found on the mainland). The two character sets have many similarities, but they are different enough that on some signs in Hong Kong Disneyland, especially those that carry important messages, guests will find three written languages (English, traditional Chinese, and simplified Chinese).

The challenge of language doesn't end there. With one-third of Hong Kong Disneyland's visitors expected to come from Hong Kong itself, another third from mainland China, and the final third from countries throughout Southeast Asia, just which language should be used the most in the park?

And the answer is . . . well, it depends. All cast members speak Cantonese and most have a passable knowledge of English and/or Putonghua. Several of the park's attractions, including Mickey's PhilharMagic, The Many Adventures of Winnie the Pooh, and Buzz Lightyear Astro Blasters, are in English. "The Festival of the Lion King" at Theater in the Wild in Adventureland is in English with two Chinese monkey characters commenting on the action in Cantonese. "The Golden Mickeys" at the Storybook Theater in Fantasyland is in Cantonese, but the songs are in English. The Hong Kong Disneyland Railroad and the Jungle River Cruise are in all three languages (in the case of the Jungle River Cruise, Guests choose which language they prefer to hear and wait in the corresponding queue). And essential information ("Please remain seated and keep your arms, hands, feet, and legs inside the vehicle and watch your children") and park announcements are in all three languages.

Whew.

As Imagineers know all too well, having done this theme park design thing for more than fifty years, written and spoken languages are key ingredients to storytelling in the Disney parks. And if they've done their job well, you shouldn't have to

ABOVE: Dumbo soars above Fantasy at Hong Kong Disneyland.

LEFT AND BELOW: A new design for Tomorrowland makes its debut at Hong Kong Disneyland.

THESE PAGES: At Disney theme parks and resorts the world over, Main Street is Main Street, kids are kids, and cast members are always there with a warm and welcoming smile.

understand the local language to enjoy the park. Storytelling is as much visual as it is aural, and that's where Disney's Imagineers excel.

Hong Kong Disneyland is a feast for the eyes. The designs of the lands, attractions, shops and restaurants are familiar (or seem so), with layers and details that are unique to this particular park.

"We guide the guests into a complete fantasy where all the perceivable, and sometimes the imperceptible, elements contribute to the story," Morris told Melody Malmberg in the book *The Making of Hong Kong Disneyland: Magic at Work*. "Architecture, landscape, graphics, music, and colors create a cohesive, choreographed experience offering an affirmative, optimistic view of life."

So it shouldn't seem so odd, then, that the first thing a largely Chinese audience sees in Hong Kong Disneyland is a street celebrating small-town America at the turn of the last century, because Main Street, U.S.A., has come to symbolize nostalgia and reassurance in almost every language. (Besides, how many Americans are still with us who can remember what life was like at the dawn of the twentieth century? Even that concept is now mostly foreign to people in the United States.)

All the familiar elements of Main Street, U.S.A., at Disneyland are here: City Hall, the Fire Department, the Opera House, the train station, Town Square, the Emporium. There are more than a few differences, however. Some, like the brick-paved street and the bandstand in the center of Town Square, are fairly obvious. Others, like the designs of the shops and restaurants inside the familiar building facades, are less so.

"Outside, you'll see a pretty faithful interpretation of Main Street [at Disneyland]," says Morris. "But inside it's all new. America was becoming a melting pot at that time, and we're conveying the immigrant story with elaborate interior details and strong storytelling."

The stories are subtle—an Austrian immigrant "operates" the Market House Bakery, a Russian proprietor started Midtown Jewelry, a trio of Spanish brothers opened Crystal Arts—but they provided the background Imagineers needed to establish a design for each shop.

Perhaps the biggest change from Main Street at Disneyland to Main Street at Hong Kong Disneyland is the one guests will probably never (and shouldn't) notice: the way it's built. All that traditional Victorian clapboard siding, gingerbread, and accents are actually made from various non-wood products, the better to withstand Hong Kong's warm, humid, wet weather.

There are also familiar elements from Disneyland in Adventureland—Tarzan's Treehouse, the Jungle Cruise—but they've been arranged and staged in such a way that the land itself is markedly different. For instance, Tarzan's Treehouse is on an island in the middle of a river (sort of like Tom Sawyer Island at Disneyland).

The Jungle Cruise (called Jungle River Cruise here)

At Hong Kong Disneyland, Adventureland combines the familiar jungle adventures with the thrills of Frontierland. Here, the Jungle River Cruise travels on a Rivers of America–size body of water, past Tarzan's Treehouse, hungry alligators, and into the mysterious depths of the jungle.

features some familiar elements—bathing elephants, ancient ruins, mischievous gorillas, charging hippos, restless natives, and witty guides—but here the action is more "in-your-face." The hippos not only charge the boats, they burp at them (nice of them to let us know they had garlic for their last meal). The natives not only shout at us, they blow lethal darts our way. The skippers' jokes are not only corny; they're corny in three languages.

The whole thing is capped off by a rumbling finale in which the fire and water gods decide to settle their differences—with guests caught in the middle. It's sort of a miniature version of the Disney Studios' Catastrophe Canyon.

Adventureland's biggest show—"The Festival of the Lion King" in the 2,626-seat Theater in the Wild—shows that the Disneyland–style parks aren't the only source of inspiration for Hong Kong Disneyland. "Festival" is an adaptation of a similar theater-in-the-round show at Disney's Animal Kingdom. Though this one has some new elements, including a rotating, elevating stage and the aforementioned pair of monkeys who comment on the action in Cantonese, the singing, dancing, storytelling, and characters are pure *Lion King*.

Fantasyland is filled with classic Disney park attractions, both old and new. There are old-time favorites—Dumbo the Flying Elephant, Cinderella Carousel, the Mad Hatter Teacups—and popular adventures of more recent vintage—The Many Adventures of Winnie the Pooh and *Mickey's PhilharMagic*.

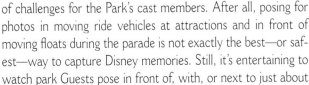

There is one brand-new attraction unique to Hong Kong Disneyland, which addresses head-on the Chinese penchant for picture taking. Fantasy Gardens, set in a parklike environment of *Fantasia* character topiaries, shade trees, and flowing stream beds of flowers, consists of five pavilions in which Disney characters greet guests, sign autographs, provide hugs and, of course, pose for pictures. The most popular Disney characters, not surprisingly, are the Fab Five (Mickey, Minnie, Donald, Goofy, and Pluto) and Winnie the Pooh, but right on their heels is Marie, the kitten from the 1970 Disney animated feature *The Aristocats*. This may be because Marie has a passing resemblance to another incredibly popular cat character in Asia (can you say hello, kitty?).

By the way, it's hard to convey the eagerness and zealousness with which visitors to Hong Kong Disneyland snap photos. Anything and everything is fair game and it's caused its share of challenges for the Park's cast members. After all, posing for photos in moving ride vehicles at attractions and in front of moving floats during the parade is not exactly the best—or safest—way to capture Disney memories. Still, it's entertaining to watch park Guests pose in front of, with, or next to just about anything that's remotely related to a Disney character. One amateur photographer took a photo of his girlfriend buying a Mickey Mouse ice cream bar, posing with the bar in the package, posing with the bar out of its package and, finally, eating the bar. (And here we thought our friends' and relatives' vacation photos were difficult to sit through.)

By necessity, Tomorrowland is the one land that bears the least resemblance to those at the other Disney parks. Though the attractions—Space Mountain, Orbitron, Buzz Lightyear Astro Blasters—are familiar, the setting had to be something other than Walt Disney's original idea of Tomorrowland as a city of the future.

"The question we asked ourselves going into this," says Tim Delaney, the Walt Disney Imagineering executive designer who led the team that created Tomorrowland, "was how do you do tomorrow when Hong Kong *is* tomorrow? It already is a futuristic city."

The answer was to forget the city-of-the-future concept and create an out-of-this-world spaceport, a place that celebrates the idea of space exploration and adventure. "All of the attractions are space-themed," says Delaney, "so the land really lent itself to this concept."

Despite the fact that its design owes a lot to the original Disneyland in California, Hong Kong Disneyland is not simply an American theme park in Asia. Respect for the traditions of Chinese culture is reflected in the layout of the Park, the design of attractions, shops, restaurants, and the two hotels, and in the park's entertainment and operation.

In addition to the use of the three different languages in attractions and on signs, Hong Kong Disneyland features local cuisine in nearly all of its restaurants. Those looking for a burger and fries will find them (the Starliner Diner in Tomorrowland serves up Western favorites, as well as the immensely popular *char siew* pork burger on a *mantau* bun), but Hong Kong Disneyland guests are more likely to find food closer to home; namely dim sum, noodles, barbecue, and stir-fry.

Not only that, because the Park is expected to draw visitors from throughout China, several of the restaurants specialize in regional cuisine: Great Northwest cooking at Clopin's Festival of Foods in Fantasyland, a menu influenced by the flavors of the Jiang Nan Region at the Comet Café in Tomorrowland, and South Asian and Guangdong-style entrees at the Tahitian Terrace restaurant in Adventureland.

Hong Kong Disneyland is also home to a classic Chinese restaurant, the Plaza Inn, situated on Main Street, U.S.A. So what's a Chinese restaurant doing at that address? Glad you asked.

The "backstory" (Imagineering-speak for the fictional story that serves as the basis for the restaurant) is that a wealthy local couple, longtime residents of Main Street, traveled to China and

fell in love with the country and its culture and cuisine. When they returned to "America," they brought with them furniture, paintings, lanterns, sculptures, and other furnishings, which they used to convert their traditional Victorian house into a "East meets West" Chinese dim sum restaurant serving authentic Cantonese and regional dishes. (The restaurant is operated by the Maxim's Group, the premier food-and-beverage company in Hong Kong.)

Another "local" element to the Park is how the ancient Chinese philosophy of feng shui helped shape the design of the Hong Kong Disneyland Resort. Feng shui (literally "wind water") is related to the belief that living *with* rather than *against* nature benefits both humans and their environment.

"Our parks combine beloved Disney characters and world-renowned stories with respect for local cultural elements to ensure guests feel at home and fully enjoy the Disney entertainment experience," says Wing Chao, master planner of architecture and design for Disney parks and resorts. "That's why we used a feng shui master on Hong Kong Disneyland. He gave us guidance on placement and balance, and, though he advised us to make several specific adjustments, I'm pleased to say that the design of this resort, based on our experience of developing four other resorts and ten parks worldwide, was already based on solid, sensible design principles, something the feng shui master readily acknowledged."

Among the principles Disney Imagineers kept in mind as they designed the Park and the Resort were carefully orienting the entire project so that it took advantage of the local

topography (principally, the "green dragon" and the "white tiger," the two hills that surround Hong Kong Disneyland); orienting the entrance to the Park to maximize energy and guest flow, which normally translates into success; the use of water throughout the resort, both as geographic (lakes, streams) and ornamental (waterfalls, fountains) features; and the strategic placement of two boulders (unseen by Park visitors) to promote stability and ensure that good fortune does not flow out of the back of the park.

Feng shui rocks were also placed in the landscaped courtyard/pool areas of the two resort hotels, which is unique in Hong Kong because there aren't that many hotels that have landscaped courtyards and expansive pool areas. In a city filled with high-rise business hotels, the low-slung, land-rich, family-friendly Hong Kong Disneyland and its resort hotels truly stand out.

The 400-room Disneyland Hotel is the flagship of the resort, featuring Victorian-style architecture, including towering turrets and gabled, red-shingled roofs. The six-story hotel features a pair of restaurants: the family-oriented Enchanted Garden Restaurant, with its buffets and tableside visits by the Disney characters; and the sophisticated Crystal Lotus, serving classic Cantonese cuisine, as well as a few Western favorites, in a setting that harmoniously balances the five elements—earth, fire, water, metal, and wood—to create the ultimate homage to feng shui (the restaurant also boasts a bevy of brand-new innovations developed by the Imagineers, including a virtual koi pond, complete with computer-animated fish that scatter when diners walk on the see-through floor, and smoke-and-fire effects behind the bar that give new meaning to the term "hot beverages").

The hotel has a lounge and tea salon, a convention center with several ballrooms and meeting spaces, indoor and outdoor swimming pools, a full-service spa, two tennis courts, two presidential suites (the Walt Disney and the Roy Disney), thirteen suites, and a Mickey Mouse–inspired garden maze.

Disney's Hollywood Hotel was created as a tribute to the golden age of show business in Los Angeles. Inside the eight-story Streamline Moderne structure are 600 guest rooms, 2 restaurants, and a lounge. Outside is a piano-shaped swimming pool, and a garden courtyard designed as a miniature map of Los Angeles and Hollywood, complete with walkways named after famous streets (such as Hollywood and Sunset Boulevards) and representations of local landmarks, including the gate at the entrance to The Walt Disney Company in Burbank.

TOP: The Disneyland Hotel provides fine lodging, swimming, a convention center, and a few Disney-style surprises.

ABOVE: The Hollywood Hotel re-creates the golden age of the movies with its striking Streamline Moderne look.

With four resorts and ten parks worldwide, Disney could already claim that the sun never sets on a Disney castle, even before the opening of the new park in Hong Kong. What the Hong Kong Disneyland Resort represents is not only Disney's fifth resort and eleventh park, but its first in the world's most populous country, a continuation of the Disneyland legacy, a bellwether for the next fifty years of Disney parks—and a pretty good use for what was once Penny's Bay.

So what are the Imagineers going to do now? Do you even have to ask?

It's a Disney World, After All

Eleven parks, five resorts, four countries, three continents, too cool!

Disneyland (July 17, 1955)
The one that started it all (and the only one Walt actually walked in)

Magic Kingdom Park, Walt Disney World Resort in Florida (October 1, 1971)
Disneyland without all the mom-and-pop motels, shops, and diners right outside the main gate

Epcot, Walt Disney World (October 1, 1982)
Permanent world's fair discovers the future and showcases the world

Tokyo Disneyland (April 15, 1983)
Disney's first international park rises in the Land of the Rising Sun

Disney Studios, Walt Disney World (May 1, 1989)
Hooray for Hollywood . . . in Orlando, Florida

Disneyland Paris (neé Euro Disneyland, April 12, 1992)
Oui, oui! The magic of Disney arrives in the City of Lights

Disney's Animal Kingdom Park, Walt Disney World (April 22, 1998)
Nahtazu (get it?) but a new species of park featuring animals living, extinct, and imaginary

Disney's California Adventure Park, Disneyland Resort (February 8, 2001)
Golden times in a celebration of the Golden State

Tokyo DisneySea, Tokyo Disney Resort (September 4, 2001)
This park completes Tokyo's land and sea Disney package

Walt Disney Studios, Disneyland Resort Paris (March 16, 2002)
Lumières, appareil-photo, action! (or something like that)

Hong Kong Disneyland (September 12, 2005)
The most recent Magic Kingdom and the first in China

Go to

www.Disney.com/DisneyInsider

DISNEY IN DEPTH

Truth is often stranger than fiction.
by Monique Peterson

CHICKEN LITTLE

One of the first times I met with *Chicken Little* director Mark Dindal and producer Randy Fulmer in the summer of 2004, I couldn't help but wonder if these men were having way too much fun. It seemed like everything that could possibly go right was going right for them—as if they'd landed upon Aladdin's lamp and conjured a real genie or been sprinkled with a generous dose of pixie dust. And yet, the making of the film had withstood more than its fair share of category-five panic attacks. One thing was clear: Mark and Randy were on to something, and enjoying every minute of it.

Steven Page and Ed Robertson of the Barenaked Ladies had just finished recording their original song "One Little Slip" for the film's opening sequence and Mark and Randy could not contain their excitement. "You've got to hear this," Randy said and popped the demo tape in. As we listened, their enthusiasm was infectious. As it turned out, the song had come together so fluidly and in a matter of weeks, not months, as originally anticipated. Not only were Mark and Randy impressed with how easily the musicians "got" *Chicken Little*, but how the Barenaked Ladies worked together as a team.

This story echoes a prominent theme that had clearly emerged throughout all levels of the *Chicken Little* pipeline: a connection with the emotional core of *Chicken Little* combined with unbelievable teamwork.

This change was a far cry from the atmosphere the previous year when the Walt Disney Studio was looking at the end of a seventy-five year era in 2-D animation. Even at the start of Mark and Randy's latest collaboration since *The Emperor's New Groove* (2000), these veteran 2-D filmmakers thought they'd be making another traditionally animated film. After twenty-plus years with the Studio, Mark and Randy had seen a lot, including the tumultuous and painful changes the Studio faced as it

closed shop on its animation studios in Florida and Paris and cut their pool of animators by the hundreds. With the impending reality of rebuilding a Studio that could facilitate the creation of computer-generated (CG) films, the idea of the sky falling at Disney was no joke to many in the biz.

In truth, the more Mark and Randy related their story about how *Chicken Little* came to be, the more it became clear that this is not just a great story about a little guy who perseveres against embarrassingly staggering odds—this is a true story inspired by the *Chicken Little* team. Obviously, some facts have been changed: names, places, actual events, and so forth, but the real story is right there, at the heart of it all.

I'm not sure which part amazed me more: how much fun the crew was having or how many nightmares they'd lived through. This smiling director-producer team did not look like the battle-scarred survivors of the challenges behind the making of *Chicken Little*. This began with the rising prominence of CG technology in the animation industry. Box office numbers had been shown a steady decline in revenues for Disney's

THESE PAGES: Our hero, Chicken Little. Character design by Tom Ellery (above left) and Mark Dindal (right).

traditionally hand-drawn films, and the company could no longer justify the cost of maintaining the animation facilities or the artists necessary for such time- and labor-intensive projects. In the midst of this climate of change, Mark and Randy were in the thick of development on what they figured could very well be the last traditionally animated film the Studio would make. Discouragement was no stranger to them as they witnessed the cutbacks and cancellations of 2-D films in production.

001.2-391

In 2003, Disney decided to put *Chicken Little* (then a story about a young girl at summer camp) in the pilot seat for their first venture into 3-D animated films without Pixar. Mark and Randy hardly had time to bask in the thrill of this new opportunity when Walt Disney Feature Animation president David Stainton saw the reel and, admittedly, almost started to cry. For Mark, that news ripped like a Band-Aid. He and Randy faced the gargantuan challenge of reworking an entire story line as well as putting a team of filmmakers together in a medium they knew virtually nothing about.

And, like Chicken Little, they picked up the bat and stepped to the plate.

What's remarkable about how Mark and Randy weathered the storm is their spirit of creative problem solving and pressing forward with a sense of optimism and determination. More notably, the way Mark and Randy approached the art, the medium, and the creative process embraces the spirit of how Walt Disney did things. Walt was a believer in the strength of story, a visionary in animation art, and a pioneer in animation technology—all things alive and well on the *Chicken Little* set. From Mark's initial idea of drawing inspiration from children's artwork to the way he and Randy nurtured a thriving creative environment for the filmmakers, they strove to capture the unfettered perspective of a childlike approach. In many ways,

001.2-466

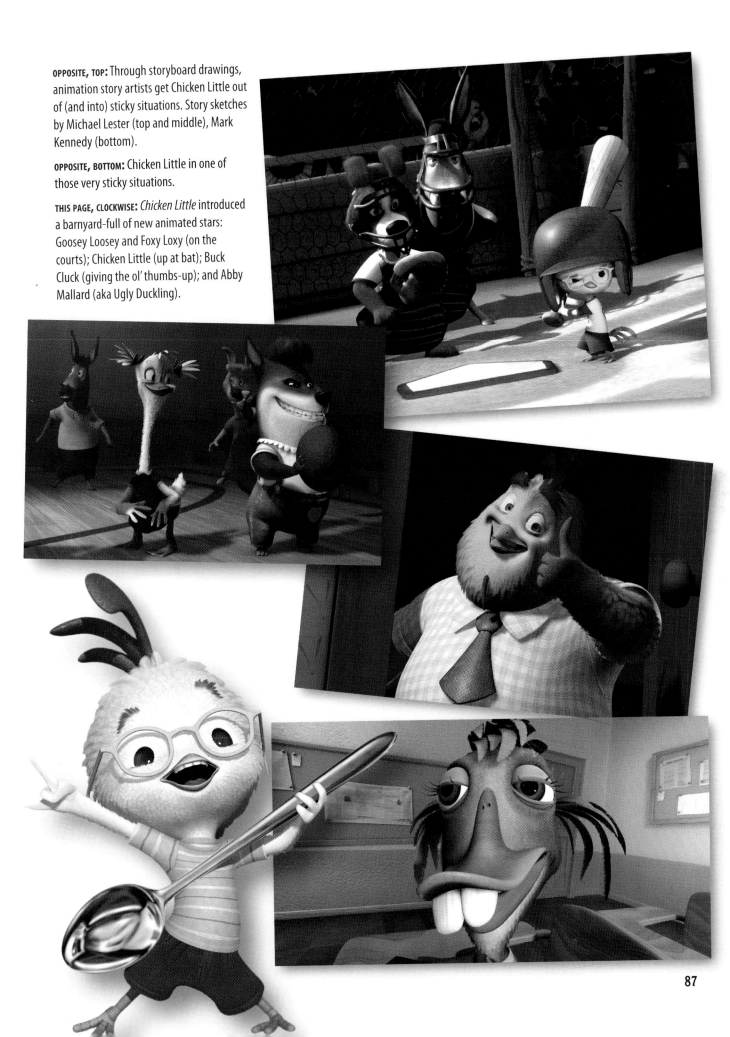

OPPOSITE, TOP: Through storyboard drawings, animation story artists get Chicken Little out of (and into) sticky situations. Story sketches by Michael Lester (top and middle), Mark Kennedy (bottom).

OPPOSITE, BOTTOM: Chicken Little in one of those very sticky situations.

THIS PAGE, CLOCKWISE: *Chicken Little* introduced a barnyard-full of new animated stars: Goosey Loosey and Foxy Loxy (on the courts); Chicken Little (up at bat); Buck Cluck (giving the ol' thumbs-up); and Abby Mallard (aka Ugly Duckling).

Chicken Little's helmsmen had no choice: they were sailing uncharted territory. Their success in bringing the *Chicken Little* team together and working with the artists has been evident in their ability to communicate their vision at a core emotional level. Randy admits, "If there's a brilliance to Mark and me, it's that we know what we know and we know what we don't know." As a result, they were able to give the filmmakers free reign in coming up with unique approaches to melding a team of 2-D and 3-D artists, and solving technical and artistic problems, as well as enhancing the art, story, and soul of the film.

The spirit that Walt infused in the company is clearly alive in a new generation of Disney filmmakers. In fact, Stephen Hunter of the *Washington Post* observed that: "The animators are—you almost no longer have to say this—fabulous and full of mischief, weaving enough ironic amusements into the story for the longer of tooth." Peter Rainer of the *Christian Science Monitor* agreed, saying: "The visuals are irrespressibly witty and so is the script, which morphs from the classic fable into a spoof of *War of the Worlds*." In the *Denver Post*, Lisa Kennedy wrote, "More than a loving, clever riff on a fable, *Chicken Little* is a grade-school primer on the language of movies with a capital *M*." Richard Corliss of *Time* magazine simply said, "It's one of the funniest, most charming, and most exhilarating movies in years."

This opening salvo for the next wave of spirited filmmaking will undoubtedly leave a permanent impression on the hearts of animation lovers of all ages and find its place in the canon of Disney's landmark classics.

Go to
Insider
www.Disney.com/DisneyInsider

ABOVE: The film's art directors give lighting and color indication for all the elements in the charming and slightly off-kilter main drag of Oakey Oaks, Chicken Little's hometown. Color key by Dan Cooper.

LEFT: Chicken Little and fellow misfits Runt of the Litter, Abby Mallard, and Fish Out of Water ponder the escalating insanity that can only mean the sky really is falling.

RIGHT: The end is near.

·THE CHRONICLES OF·
NARNIA

THE LION, THE WITCH AND THE WARDROBE

C.S. Lewis Meets Walt Disney:
Two Mythmakers Journey Into Narnia

by Brian Sibley

The Land of Narnia has been waiting to be put onto film. For fifty-five years, the inhabitants of the enchanted realm that lies between the lamppost and the great castle at Cair Paravel have awaited the moment when a film company would have the vision and the courage to step through the wardrobe door and set up their cameras.

The Walt Disney Studios and Walden Media production *The Chronicles of Narnia: The Lion, the Witch and the Wardrobe*, is based on the first of seven books written by British author, academic, and Christian essayist C. S. Lewis.

At first glance, any comparison between the Chicago-born, Missouri-raised Walt Disney and the Irish-born, Oxford-educated Clive Staples Lewis seems somewhat unlikely. However, only two years separated their births, and they lived to be almost the same age, spanning an identical era of history, albeit on opposite sides of the Atlantic. Both men achieved huge international fame, sharing the distinction of being a cover subject of *Time* magazine and voted among The 1000 Makers of the Twentieth Century.

What also unites the largely self-taught and totally visionary filmmaker and the university scholar, literary critic, and spiritual guru is their extraordinary visual imagination.

"Like Walt Disney," says Dick Cook, Chairman of the Walt Disney Studios, "C. S. Lewis was a master storyteller, and the *Narnia* books provide a treasure trove of tales to tell. Narnia is a world unlike any you've ever seen before, and because it is a Walt Disney Picture, the message will be loud and clear that this is a film for audiences of all ages."

C. S. Lewis would have appreciated this understanding, having once observed: "No book is really worth reading at the age of ten which is not equally (and often far more) worth reading at the age of fifty and beyond."

Ruled by Aslan, the great, golden-maned lion, Narnia is peopled by wonderful characters: talking animals, giants, dwarves, and an extraordinary menagerie of mythological creatures as well as a rabble of monstrous beings serving Jadis, the White Witch, who has frozen Narnia under a terrible spell that makes it always winter but never Christmas.

RIGHT: Acclaimed author and scholar C. S. Lewis created a world of wonder, adventure, and enchantment in his *Chronicles of Narnia*—a world that the filmmakers faithfully re-created in the epic film released in 2005.

Narnia is a fantastical world, parallel to our own which—on rare occasions—can be entered via doors in *this* world. In *The Lion, the Witch and the Wardrobe*, four children—Peter, Susan, Edmund, and Lucy Pevensie—find their way into a land caught up in a desperate struggle between the forces of good and evil to the extent that their own lives and destinies become entangled with those of the peoples of Narnia, and their courage and loyalty are dramatically put to the test.

Writing of the origins of Narnia, Lewis explained: "At first they were not a story, just pictures." There was one picture in particular, "of a faun carrying an umbrella and parcels in a snowy wood," that had been in Lewis's mind since he was sixteen years old, waiting, as it were, to be explained. "Then, one day," he recalled, "I said to myself, 'Let's try and make a story about it.'"

At first, Lewis wasn't sure how the story would develop but then, suddenly, "Aslan came bounding in!" he confessed: "I don't know where the Lion came from or why He came. But once He was there, He pulled the whole story together."

On their original publication in the 1950s, the *Chronicles of Narnia* were immediately hailed as modern classics of children's literature: a status they have never lost, becoming the best-loved books for several generations of young readers.

This reputation (reinforced by the fact that the series is second only to *Harry Potter* in international popularity) meant that the film of *The Lion, the Witch and the Wardrobe* was eagerly anticipated with, for fans, the usual attendant fears about how faithfully the story would be translated from page to screen. They need not have worried. From the moment audiences got their initial glimpse of Aslan's kingdom in the first trailer through enthusiastic reports from test screenings, it was clear that the filmmakers had not only met but had surpassed the Narnia-lovers' exacting expectations.

That it has taken five and a half decades for *The Lion, The Witch and the Wardrobe* to reach our cinemas, despite interest from various Hollywood filmmakers over the years, is due in no small measure to the challenges presented by such a project. To create the world of Narnia and to convincingly people it with such hybrid characters as fauns, centaurs, minotaurs, and gryphons would have made creative demands that could not have been met before now.

Film series such as *The Lord of the Rings* have paved the way for a sophisticated and believable depiction of the impossible. In *The Lion, the Witch and the Wardrobe*, thanks to advanced movie technology harnessed by Hollywood effects houses Sony Imageworks, Rhythm & Hues, and Industrial Light & Magic, as well as the geniuses of New Zealand's WETA Workshop, film effects have achieved new heights.

THESE PAGES: A magical world of unicorns, snow queens, and eternal winter await Peter, Susan, Edmund, and Lucy beyond the secret wardrobe.

93

Fantasy in the cinema has become the new realism.

Stunning effects aside, the enthusiastic response to *The Lion, the Witch and the Wardrobe* is, as much as anything, the result of an unswerving commitment on the part of production company Walden Pictures, who secured the rights to the *Narnia* books, and their partners Walt Disney Studios to make a film that was "true to the word."

That initial pledge was confirmed in the decision to appoint Andrew Adamson to direct the film. Although Adamson established his directorial credentials in the field of animation with the hugely successful *Shrek* and *Shrek 2*, he had long harboured an ambition to film the stories of Narnia, having read and fallen in love with C. S. Lewis's books as a boy. His stated aim to "make a movie inspired by my memory of the book as an eight-year-old" was, perhaps, the best safeguard any Narnia aficionado could have wished for.

"People won't write the books I want," C. S. Lewis once said, " so I have to do it for myself." As a result, readers of the Narnian septet develop their own intensely personal relationship with the books, revisiting them over the years, either for their own pleasure or to share the experience with children and grandchildren; drawn back again and again by those compelling images that first inspired Lewis's writing.

Walt Disney also possessed a unique ability to see stories in terms of pictures. His immediate response to the books that he read—from *Pinocchio* to *Mary Poppins*—was to see them in terms of potential film imagery and that was how he then worked on interpreting those stories for the screen.

One has only to read the notes of the many story conferences which Walt held with his writers and animators to see how he conjured image after image—sometimes comic, sometimes emotional or dramatic—that would eventually shape the creation of some of the most memorable Disney sequences to find their way onto film.

This was Walt Disney's personal, and often underrated, contribution to his studio's animated pictures. It was also the legacy that he bequeathed to a company dedicated to telling visually exciting stories.

Although there can be few stories more exciting than *The Lion, the Witch and the Wardrobe*, this is not simply one wonderful story, it is only the first of C. S. Lewis's repeatedly magical excursions into Narnia. As such, it offers Disney the chance to develop a multiyear franchise that, in turn, will provide moviegoers with an ongoing opportunity to enter a realm of unforgettable enchantment.

www.Disney.com/DisneyInsider

96

Previous Explorations of Narnia

The Lion, the Witch and the Wardrobe began for author C. S. Lewis as pictures in the mind, including "a queen on a sledge" and "a magnificent lion." Small wonder the stories have captured so many creative imaginations. Beginning with the first drawings by Pauline Baynes, perfectly capturing the images in Lewis's head, the book has been illustrated and decorated by various artists.

And while, until now, the books have eluded the attention of feature filmmakers, they have been interpreted in various other creative media, from recordings on disc by such storytellers as Claire Bloom and Kenneth Branagh to elaborately staged theatre productions.

The complete *Chronicles* have twice been presented, to great acclaim, as radio dramatizations: first by the BBC and more recently by "Focus on the Family" for broadcast in America.

The *Chronicles* have also been popularly adapted for television, beginning in 1967 with a British serialization of *The Lion, the Witch and the Wardrobe* by ABC Weekend Television. The book was next televised in 1979 as an Emmy Award–winning, animated special for CBS-TV directed by Bill Melendez, creator of the popular Charlie Brown cartoon films. Then, in 1988, the BBC produced a new television version of *The Lion*, which won a British Academy Award and was followed by adaptations of three more of the *Chronicles*.

Now comes the first-ever Narnia feature film with a cast headed by Tilda Swinton, James McAvoy, Jim Broadbent, and James Cosmo and a lineup of voice talents that includes Rupert Everett, Ray Winstone, Dawn French, and Liam Neeson as Aslan.

DISNEY'S TARZAN SOARS ONTO BROADWAY

*When Disney's animated film **Tarzan** opened in American movie theaters in 1999, the iconic character of the noble ape man was already eighty-eight years old. Edgar Rice Burroughs wrote the first of his twenty-six Tarzan books in 1911; **Tarzan of the Apes** was published, serial-style, beginning in the October 1912 issue of The All-Story Magazine. The first of almost fifty Tarzan films made its debut in New York City in 1918, with Elmo Lincoln as Tarzan, and was the first film ever to sell $1 million worth of tickets.*

by Michael Lassell

In September 2005, Disney Theatrical Productions announced the return of Tarzan—only this time in a brand-new Broadway musical. The company that introduced an animated Tarzan—a character who sailed through the jungle canopy with the extreme-sports moves of surfing and skateboarding—would reinvent the tale once again. To start the long development process, Thomas Schumacher, president of Disney Theatrical Productions, went back to the source material to find the essential story. There is a reason that almost all of Disney's classic films begin with a book opening: in all of Disney's enterprises, from its films to its theme park attractions, the focus is always on the *story*.

Schumacher went back to the original *Tarzan of the Apes*, an adventure tale written for a predominantly adult male audience. Some of the material would never translate into family entertainment, but he found in the Burroughs text the essential tale of Tarzan for a modern audience, the underlying reason, he believes, that

generations of adults and children have found the fiction so compelling.

"The story of Tarzan," Schumacher said at the first announcement of the "Tarzan" stage project, "is the story of family. It's the story of an individual, in this case Tarzan, who needs to find out where he belongs. It's the story of anyone who has ever felt like a misfit, the story of anyone who has had to find his or her place in the world.

"Ultimately," he told the rapt audience, "Tarzan comes to understand his own identity and to understand the meaning of family—the family of man, to which he was born, the family of the apes who raised him, and the family he makes himself, which includes both Jane and the jungle creatures he loves."

Schumacher, whose other work experience includes mounting citywide avant-garde performing arts festivals in Los Angeles (including one for the Olympics in 1984), is also the former president of Disney Feature Animation, where he supervised the production of twenty-one animated films including *The Lion King*, *Lilo & Stitch*, *Tarzan*, and *Mulan*. Given his background, he is no stranger to the connection between stage and film. He produced the original stage productions of "The Lion King" and "Aida," with music by Elton John and Tim Rice, and "Mary Poppins," and oversaw Disney's "Beauty and the Beast"—all among the most successful productions in Broadway history.

One of the essential differences between an animated family film and a Broadway musical is its length. Films are typically far shorter than the Broadway-stage norm. Disney's on-the-boards "Tarzan" is comprised of two full acts and an intermission, nearly twice the length of the animated film. This presented both a challenge and an opportunity. To refocus and expand the story, Schumacher turned to Tony-winning playwright (and opera librettist) David Henry Hwang.

Hwang, who also contributed to the book for Disney's "Aida," wrote a new script that incorporated elements from Edgar Rice Burroughs's *Tarzan of the Apes*; the Disney animated screenplay created by Tab Murphy and Bob Tzudiker & Noni White; and entirely new material created for the stage production. Some story points remain the same, such as the way Tarzan learns to speak the English language. In Burroughs's novel, Tarzan teaches himself to speak from the books his parents brought with them from home. In the animated film, it is Jane who teaches Tarzan his "native tongue," as she does in the stage version. There are also some differences, too. In the Disney film, Jane is an artist and anthropologist; on stage, she has been transformed into an adventurous botanist.

To translate the story to stage, it was also necessary to conceive a theatrical reality that would differentiate it from the film. The Broadway musical version of "Tarzan" that plays the Richard Rodgers Theatre would have to be,

for aesthetic as well as practical reasons, very different from Disney's own film, although, of course, there would be similarities. While the film and stage versions feature both a younger and an older Tarzan, a large number of apes, and a tension between the "two worlds" of ape and man, there are differences, too—in the role of Clayton, the hunter, and in the elimination of some characters from the film who did not seem as necessary for the stage version as they did for the movie.

To create the music of the new show, Schumacher made the obvious choice. British rocker Phil Collins not only won an Academy Award for "You'll Be in My Heart," one of the five songs he wrote for the Disney film *Tarzan*, he also won a Grammy Award for the sound track album. Collins was also eager to work on Broadway. A drummer from the time he was five, Collins started his professional career as a singing and dancing actor (he played the Artful Dodger in the original West End production of "Oliver!" in 1963). In the course of working on the show score, he created eight new songs and has revisited the original five: "Two Worlds," "You'll Be in My Heart," "Son of Man," "Trashin' the Camp," and "Strangers Like Me."

ABOVE: Josh Strickland and Jenn Gambatese—aka Tarzan and Jane—join songwriter Phil Collins for the announcement of "Tarzan," the Broadway musical.

LEFT: Phil Collins (right) and president of Disney Theatrical Productions Thomas Schumacher take the stage for an impromptu concert.

Unlike prior Disney films, in which the songs were sung by the characters, in the *Tarzan* film, Collins himself sang all five songs as a sort of narrator. Naturally, for the stage version, the characters themselves sing, including both the boy and man Tarzan, Jane, and the apes.

Visually, Schumacher wanted a specifically theatrical production, and so, for his production team, he turned to people whose work he admired. Bob Crowley, an Irish-born, British designer and associate for the Royal National Theater (who has also designed for the Royal Shakespeare Company, the Royal Ballet, and the Royal Opera at Covent Garden) has had great success creating sets and costumes for Broadway, winning his second Tony Award for the stunning sets for Disney's "Aida." Then Schumacher made one of his characteristic risky moves: he signed Crowley on to direct the production as well.

"Bob has a great conceptual understanding of structure," Schumacher says. "He is a poet of stage design and seems to understand theatrical reality as a birthright. He was a natural choice, especially as we moved forward, and it became clear that the design of this production would be more intimately related to the action of the story and the movements of the actors than is usual. Bob sees the big picture."

The big picture that Schumacher and Crowley revealed at the September "first peek" event was highly unexpected. The set, representing the mysterious, carefree, and treacherous jungle—from canopy to roots—would be abstracted to purely theatrical gestures to invite the audience's imagination to finish the reality. Costumes would also be pared down to the essentials. They would refer to apes, for example, but make no attempt to imitate them. Those abstract, morphing sets and suggestive costumes would be enhanced by lighting from the unparalleled Natasha Katz, who also won a Tony Award for her work on "Aida."

Schumacher is the man who hired cutting-edge stage and film director and designer Julie Taymor to direct Disney's stage version of "The Lion King," one of the most potentially risky but ultimately successful decisions ever made by a theatre producer. He had similar surprises for the creative team of "Tarzan." Choreography for "Tarzan" was assigned to the great Australian dancer and choreographer Meryl Tankard, whom Schumacher had first seen in the early 1980s, when she was the featured soloist in the groundbreaking Pina Bausch Wuppertaler Tanztheater. She also performed at the Olympic Arts Festival in Los Angeles in 1984.

Working with Tankard would be another surprising individual, Pichón Baldinu, the Argentine stage visionary who created the famous De La Guarda Company. His particular brand of theatrical invention involves suspending

actors from the ceiling, singly and *en masse*. It was a perfect metaphoric approach for the apes of the Broadway "Tarzan." They would fly and climb on a giant jungle gym from thick elastic cords. If the underlying movements of the animated *Tarzan* were inspired by surfing and snowboarding; the movement of the stage show would be based on bungee jumping and rock climbing. Actors would fly through the air—not on thin wires audiences must pretend not to see (as in "Peter Pan")—but on visible ropes attached to harnesses that are part of the actors' costumes.

Earlier in 2005, Schumacher, Crowley, and the rest of the creative team traveled to Buenos Aires to observe, oversee, and participate in what can be described as an "aerial exploration" of "Tarzan." In an abandoned theater in a rundown district of the South American city, and using performers from his own company, Baldinu explored the idea of a theatrical movement language for the singing and dancing ensemble of "apes" in the show. Working from a makeshift superstructure, the performers (and on at least one occasion Schumacher himself) climbed and flew around the set.

Using what the creative team learned from its exercises in Argentina made casting the show an adventure. Yes, the actors had to come into a studio to sing for the producers, the director, and music producer Paul Bogaev, but they had to do it while hanging ten feet in mid-air! Bogaev's musical resume includes an Oscar for the *Chicago* film sound track, a Grammy for the "Aida" cast album, and conducting gigs for Barbra Streisand and Elton John, among others. In addition to singing while flying, the actors had to move, too—and in a very particular way.

LEFT AND BELOW: Small scale set models illustrate how Bob Crowley's innovative scenic design will bring the Disney animated classic to life on Broadway.

Actors in safety helmets were attached to their bungee cords and set loose to explore movement in whatever way they wanted to improvise, while an expanded version of the song "Son of Man" played on the sound system.

The audition process proved to be a learning experience for the creative team as well as for the actors hoping to be in the show. "It's amazing how much you can tell about a dancer from watching this," said Bob Crowley at the time. "You can see how comfortable they are with the flying, with the height and the sense of danger, and how free they are with their bodies, how much they enjoy the freedom. You can base a lot of casting decisions on things like that."

As the script, music, choreography, aerial movement, set design, and casting all continued to develop prior to the beginning of formal rehearsals, Schumacher and the creative team realized that they needed to further explore the complex relationship between these crucial elements of the show. Since some new adventures were being invented for the story, and since they involved integrating the set, the costumes, and the actors, the logistics of flying had to be sketched out, if not finalized, before the final set was designed or built. So, in July 2005, Disney Theatrical Productions held its own "aerial lab" as an extension of Baldinu's work in Argentina earlier in the year. Performers offered a glimpse at how flying entrances and exits could be made, how the show's exotic animals (such as the blood-thirsty leopard, Sabor) would be portrayed, and how scenes in which the set and the actors interact (the shipwreck, the building of the tree house, and so forth) could be accomplished. The aerial-lab process proved to be a smart move: a number of theatrical moments were discovered over the course of the lab, and, by the end of the process, the creative team felt certain that the elements of the show would ultimately come together in a cohesive way—in other words, they felt that an exciting and innovative new musical was on its way to Broadway.

Rehearsals began in January 2006. Because of the special movement requirements of this production, it was clear throughout the development process that it would not hold rehearsals in a typical studio. The entire rehearsal process would instead have to take place in a space big enough to hold the stage rigging for the flying. The production team at DTP found an unusual location—Steiner Studios, a motion picture studio in Brooklyn, New York—for its rehearsals. There, the creative team and cast continued to explore and create this new piece of Broadway history. The long journey of the development of "Tarzan," the Broadway musical, resulted in its world premiere in March 2006, and will soon be followed by its opening night on May 10, 2006—almost one hundred years after Burroughs first introduced the character!

CAPTAIN JACK IS BACK!
THE NEW VOYAGES OF
PIRATES OF THE CARIBBEAN

by *Jason Surrell*

At this point in movie history, nobody in Hollywood spews coffee all over the front page of *Variety* when films about boy wizards and moody young men in tights and capes—or anything with *Star Wars* or *Lord of the Rings* in the title—make hundreds of millions of dollars at the box office. Movies based on amusement park rides, however, aren't given that same benefit of the doubt; at least they weren't three years ago, when *Pirates of the Caribbean: The Curse of the Black Pearl* sailed onto movie screens. Although the film took audiences and the industry by surprise, it came as a vindication to the handful of filmmakers and Disney studio executives that knew they had something special on their hands after an early test screening. "The first preview was spectacular," recalled Nina Jacobson, president, Buena Vista Motion Pictures Group. "That's when we knew, when we went to that first screening. The second they saw the dog in the cell and started laughing—that's when we knew it was going to be more than a movie. It was going to be a cultural phenomenon."

The film's "unlikely" success was especially welcome considering that Jacobson and Walt Disney Studios chairman Dick Cook had been championing the project from the moment senior vice president production Brigham Taylor and his team first pitched the idea in a page-and-a-half memo back in the summer of 2000. "Dick and I really believed in it from the beginning," Nina recalled. "We had faith. Now, we may have been completely out of our minds, but we thought it would work."

Not only did it "work," *Pirates of the Caribbean: The Curse of the Black Pearl* ultimately became the highest grossing live-action film in the history of Walt Disney Pictures. It became a bona fide cultural phenomenon, and it did so utilizing a property with its feet firmly planted in Disney's storied past—which could not have been more fitting, according to Nina Jacobson. "Pirates of the Caribbean is something that started with Walt Disney and still had the cultural relevance to become a phenomenon. This film is based on something that came directly from Walt's brain, and that's incredibly cool."

What didn't come as a surprise to the rest of the industry was the green light the Walt Disney Studios gave producer Jerry Bruckheimer and director Gore Verbinski for not one but two additional films, creating both an instant franchise and a trilogy that tells one epic story.

And so in the fall of 2004, screenwriters Ted Elliott and Terry Rossio returned to the keyboard to chronicle the further adventures of Captain Jack Sparrow (Johnny Depp), Will Turner (Orlando Bloom), and Elizabeth Swann (Keira Knightley), reuniting them with old friends and pitting them against old foes—along with enemies that have yet to reveal themselves.

Ted and Terry's office on the first floor of Walt's original Animation Building on the Disney Studio lot became a repository of pirate lore as they brainstormed ideas for the new voyages of Captain Jack Sparrow. Index cards covered an entire wall of their office, outlining scenes and story lines that would span two films. Some of the ideas—the inclusion of a giant sea monster, for example—would make it into the final scripts; others—such as a stop in the Disneyland-inspired Port of New Orleans—fell by the wayside.

As more and more details fell into place, the two films made their way from twelve-page rough outlines to thirty-page treatments to full script drafts. The works in progress would circulate

THESE PAGES: The thrills continue in not one, but two new film adventures.

between Ted and Terry, producer Jerry Bruckheimer, director Gore Verbinski, and Disney studio executive Nina Jacobson. As everyone agreed on certain story points, Gore worked with production designer Rick Heinrichs (*Lemony Snicket's A Series of Unfortunate Events*) and a team of artists, many of them veterans of the first film, to bring those ideas to life in a series of evocative concept sketches.

Dead Man's Chest picks up where the first film left off, with Captain Jack reunited with the crew of the *Black Pearl*, and the engaged Elizabeth and Will both wanted for piracy by the British Crown. We finally meet Will's father, Bootstrap Bill (Stellan Skarsgard), and there's a *new* enemy gunning for Sparrow: the infamous Davy Jones (Bill Nighy) himself, captain of the ghost ship *Flying Dutchman*, and his own crew of the damned. Deals are made and broken, allegiances shift like island sands, and the story concludes with the one-two punch of a jaw-dropping cliff-hanger and mind-altering plot twist. The saga concludes in a third *Pirates of the Caribbean* film, in which Captain Jack carries on his tradition of cheating poor fortune at every turn.

As important as it was to Ted and Terry to create two films that would stand on their own, they also wanted to ensure that the new installments flowed naturally from the first movie to create a real trilogy with a solid beginning, middle, and end. "We went back to the first movie and looked for tiny story details that we could somehow 'pay off' in the second and third films," Terry Rossio says. "We really want the three movies to feel like an organic trilogy, not a surprise hit that spawned two quickie sequels." So we'll learn the story behind Commodore Norrington's casual mention of Jack's "brush with the East India Trading Company" and Sparrow's own seemingly tall tale of how a remote island tribe once "made me their chief." And Jack's cryptic comment, "Clearly, you've never been to Singapore," will have a whole new meaning to film audiences.

Disney theme park fans will also find additional references to the attraction upon which the films are based in both *Pirates* sequels. The crowd-pleasing jailhouse dog makes an encore appearance in *Dead Man's Chest*, and a favorite setting from the Disneyland original, the Blue Bayou, is home to a major new character, voodoo priestess Tia Dalma (Naomie Harris).

With Ted and Terry on set continuing to polish the scripts inside California soundstages and on location in the Caribbean, the two films went into production back-to-back in February 2005, with *Pirates of the Caribbean: Dead Man's Chest* set for release on July 7, 2006, and the third *Pirates of the Caribbean* feature slated to follow in the summer of 2007. And if the words of Captain Jack himself are any indication, it's possible that audiences may not have seen the last of their favorite crew: "I would do *Pirates VII* if they asked me," Johnny Depp said from the set of *Dead Man's Chest*. "I just really love this character."

He's not alone.

Go to

www.Disney.com/DisneyInsider

103

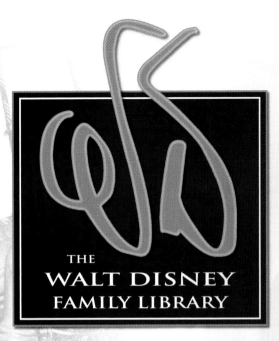

THE WALT DISNEY FAMILY LIBRARY

by Paula Sigman Lowery

"Welcome to The Walt Disney Family Library." With these words, visitors will be invited to experience a brand-new way to meet the man behind the mouse, to share in his memories, and get to know him better—and more intimately—than ever before. Now in its final concept and design phase, the Library is scheduled to open in 2008. Situated in historic 19th-century barracks buildings in one of America's national treasures, the San Francisco Presidio, the Library is sure to become a must-see destination and resource for Disney fans and film scholars alike.

The original idea of the Library, which is a project of The Walt Disney Family Foundation, was a little family office where Walt's awards, memorabilia, and memories would be showcased. Walter Elias Disney Miller, President of the Foundation and grandson of the man for whom he was named, envisioned it as a place "where we would conduct our Walt Disney Family Foundation business while surrounded by an atmosphere that was all about Walt and Lilly, family and career." They dreamed of having small groups of schoolchildren visit the office, to learn a little something about the man behind the name. But the family soon realized their idea of an office was impractical, for like another well-known "field of dreams," if you build it, they will come. How in the world could their little office/museum accommodate all the people for whom Walt Disney is important?

Meanwhile, the public's interest in Walt Disney continued to increase—as did misconceptions and misunderstandings about his life. Walter explains, "The interest in my grandpa never seems to go away. When I meet people and they learn that Walt Disney was my grandpa, usually a big warm smile comes across their face, and they tell me how much Bambi, Mickey Mouse, or Disneyland meant to them as a child growing up. People remember where they were on Sunday nights; they never forget crying during *Old Yeller*; or the thrill of running down Main Street for that first ride of the day at Disneyland. However, inevitably difficult or misunderstood questions surface: 'Is he really frozen?' 'Did he draw all of those characters?' 'Was he anti-Semitic?'" In spite of numerous books and films about the life of Walt Disney, nonsensical and even hurtful rumors continue to abound about his personal life, the way he treated his employees, and about the type of person he really was.

Walter continues, "My grandpa was an extremely curious man, and with his legacy the public has grown to be curious about him. Who is Walt Disney, and what made him so successful and talented at what he did? Yet there is a whole generation that does not know that he was a man, a very decent man: a man who worked hard all of his life, a man who loved all people, and who is much more than a corporate symbol, or a picture on toys and video packaging."

The family began taking steps to demystify Walt. In 2001 they produced a biographical CD-ROM, as well as a documentary film, *Walt: The Man Behind the Myth*. They also launched The Walt Disney Family Museum, a virtual museum, hosted online by The Walt Disney Company at www.waltdisney.org. Curators Richard and Katherine Greene and Pantheon

We keep moving forward, opening new doors, and doing new things, because we're curious, and curiosity keeps leading us down new paths."

Walt Disney

BELOW: Scheduled to open in 2008 at the historic Presidio of San Francisco, The Walt Disney Family Library will offer visitors a fascinating look at a fascinating man.

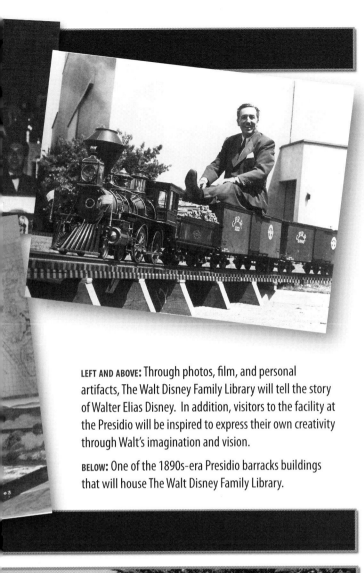

LEFT AND ABOVE: Through photos, film, and personal artifacts, The Walt Disney Family Library will tell the story of Walter Elias Disney. In addition, visitors to the facility at the Presidio will be inspired to express their own creativity through Walt's imagination and vision.

BELOW: One of the 1890s-era Presidio barracks buildings that will house The Walt Disney Family Library.

Productions (who also produced the film documentary) update the site regularly with news, feature articles, and exclusive interviews. Still, the family felt they could do more.

They returned to the thought of a physical museum. Walter concedes their original vision was too limited: "We realized this library needed to provide much more than what we had envisioned, because the public would demand it, and they would appreciate it." He also believed that Walt Disney deserved it.

By this time, it had also become an intensely personal mission for Walt Disney's daughter, Diane Disney Miller. "Through the process of doing the CD-ROM and the film," she says, "I have a larger awareness of how important my dad is to so many people, in a very positive way. It has been very humbling to me."

Exposing the rumors, misconceptions, and—in Diane's words—"malicious inventions" that were created and twisted to sensationalize her father's life story was just the beginning. "I never thought that I'd have to do anything like this," she confesses. "I believed that my father's legacy was well cared for by the Company. I have complete faith and trust in [Walt Disney Archives director] Dave Smith and the staff that he has selected and works with in the Walt Disney Archives. Dave deals with nothing but the truth, and is as outraged about abuse of the facts of my father's life as I am."

But Diane recognized that Dave Smith and The Walt Disney Company had broader responsibilities. It was time for the family to make its bold move. "What began as a defensive action became something much grander," she explains. "We are not just doing it for my dad now, but for everyone everywhere to whom Disney is important. His work, his product, has brought so much joy and inspiration to so many that it is important that we create this library and make it entertaining, illuminating, and accessible to everyone."

To that end, the family is delving into their personal family albums, home movies, and family treasures to help bring Walt Disney's story to life. One of the family's biggest challenges has been recognizing that although their original artifact holdings were important, they were limited in scope. There are hundreds of awards and honors that had been presented to Walt Disney, including his acclaimed Academy Award for the creation of Mickey Mouse, and the special Academy Award for *Snow White and the Seven Dwarfs* that consists of one large Oscar and seven little ones. There is Walt Disney's personal memorabilia, including his father's fiddle. There are the miniatures he began collecting on his trips around the world. The family has his special train, the *Lilly Belle*. But there was something key to the Walt Disney story that the family didn't have. Diane reveals, "We had no animation art. My family didn't possess any. My dad didn't bring it home."

Without a strong collection of Disney art, Diane's original concept was to concentrate on telling Walt's story through interviews, films, and his own presence. Walt was so

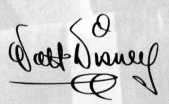

"We have always tried to be guided by the basic idea that, in the discovery of knowledge, there is great entertainment—as, conversely, in all good entertainment there is always some grain of wisdom, humanity, or enlightenment to be gained."

thoroughly photographed and filmed throughout his life that the Library has an unmatched archive of images from which to choose. The Walt Disney Company also recognizes the value of the Library, and is providing access to cherished images and materials. Additionally, the Library is gathering information and undertaking oral and video histories with the artists and other key players who knew and worked with Walt. These histories, to be maintained in the Library's research and reference collections, will provide authors, historians, and researchers with a wealth of information unavailable elsewhere.

Thus, the family's initial dream of a small museum expanded in scope: its mission is to present the life and career of Walt Disney in an honest and entertaining manner, with a library and archive that will fulfill the needs of serious scholars of the man, his work, and his times.

The Library's story team came up with a track that allows the exhibits to concentrate on Walt's personal story, rather than that of the company he founded (although they are indeed intertwined). The Library's permanent presentation will showcase a "chronology of big ideas" that shaped the philosophy, career, contributions, and legacy of the man regarded as the master showman of the twentieth century.

When asked how the family will accomplish this, Walter Miller is quick to answer. "We hope to tell the story of the man during his life, through his own voice, his family, friends, employees, historians, scholars, and those who were close to him. We want to give the public his life story by those who knew him best." He has specific goals for the project: "I feel personally that I owe him so much, as a grandson who admires his grandpa, but mostly for what he gave to the world in his short life. We hope this library will give to the visiting public an experience that they will hold onto emotionally . . . something to grasp onto and leave with, learn from, be inspired by, and have a sense of accomplishment and inspiration as they walk out the doors. Or, simply, to understand what he was about and how he went about it."

The Library has also begun building a collection of animation art that will be useful in telling Walt's story. Still, even more important than the images and artifacts are the stories behind them. "The art is beautiful, but it's more important to get the words," notes Diane. "The truth is so important to me. Not an exaggeration or a beautification of his life."

The Library expects to offer visitors a chance to observe "a day in the life of Walt Disney," both at work and at home. It will present the story of Walt's life in the context of the world in which he lived. It is also the story of the men and women with whom he worked. And it is the story of the people—artists and astronauts, fans and filmmakers, scientists, and even urban planners—who were inspired by his life's work, and continue to carry on his legacy today.

Assisting the Family Foundation is a cadre of noted historians and filmmakers, teachers and scholars, including

J.B. Kaufman, Charles Solomon, John Canemaker, Leonard Maltin, John Lasseter, Dick Cook, Ted and Kuniko Thomas, Jean-Pierre Isbouts and Cathie Labrador of Pantheon Productions, and Richard and Katherine Greene. Walter couldn't be more pleased: "We have a great team in place. Jeff Kurtti [Disney historian, author, and documentarian], Bruce Gordon [author, designer, and former Disney Imagineer] and Paula Sigman Lowery [former Disney archivist and writer] make up the story and content team. With them on board, we have found a new direction and are finally moving forward with a team that not only knows the story, but also admires and respects the story and the man behind it. Jay Turnbull [of San Francisco–based Page & Turnbull, a renowned and respected architectural, historic preservation, and urban-design firm] and his colleagues, Dave Roccosalva and Carolyn Kiernat, are a guiding force that will let the building help dictate what we do within it." Other members of the team include project manager Tom Kipling; collections manager Michael Labrie; legal guru Charles Wixson; and another former Imagineer, Hugh Chitwood, who serves as media research specialist. Walter concludes, "As my grandpa did time and again, he handpicked the team and made it work. I believe now . . . we have the team in place to make this Library the best it can be."

In searching for a site for their project, the Disney family considered a number of options. There was a brief thought of displaying the Academy Awards at the Walt Disney Concert Hall in Los Angeles. They considered the Griffith Park area of Burbank/Glendale, but that turned out to be the perfect spot for Walt Disney's barn (relocated from his home in Holmby Hills). The idea of Kansas City's Union Station—set for historic renovation—came up. Then Diane and husband Ron Miller, who live in San Francisco, heard that its famed Presidio was closing as an Army base and might be leasing some of its historic buildings in the spirit of civic rehabilitation. The Presidio was once the U.S. Army's premier West Coast base, serving the nation in that role from 1846 until the 1990s, when it was transferred to the National Park Service as a National Historic Landmark District. Part of the Golden Gate National Recreation Area, it is the world's largest national park in an urban setting. When Ron and Diane visited the Presidio, they saw its potential. As a home for the Walt Disney Family Library, it seemed just right. San Francisco is an international city with great public transportation, so it would be an easy destination for visitors. But even more importantly, the idea of preserving a historic structure, putting something wonderful inside, and giving it new life is something Diane felt her father would have loved. And they're helping to develop one of the country's newest national parks.

Walter agrees: "It truly is one of the most beautiful locations in the world. With the Pacific at our feet and the great city of San Francisco at our door, it is a perfect fit. I love that you can stroll down to the water's edge, hike through a

ABOVE AND BELOW: Walt Disney enjoyed spending time at Disneyland, whether staying in his apartment above the firehouse or cannon-balling an authentic steam locomotive along the "Circle Route" around the perimeter of the Park. Walt always greeted Guests with a warm and friendly smile.

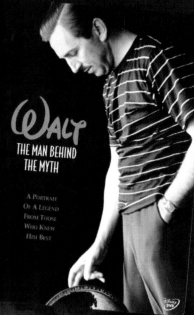

THIS PAGE: One of the important missions of The Walt Disney Family Library will be its ongoing outreach and education programs for children and young adults. The ideas and techniques already presented in film, publishing, Internet, and CD form will be expanded, all with Walt's vast creative heritage at the center.

Courage

is the main quality of leadership, in my opinion, no matter where it is exercised. Usually it implies some risk—especially in new undertakings. Courage to initiate something and to keep it going— pioneering and adventurous spirit to blaze new ways, often, in our land of opportunity.

eucalyptus forest, visit the Golden Gate bridge, or picnic on the parade grounds . . . all by foot from our Library door."

The Library will continue the legacy of Walt Disney, not only to share the truth of his life, but also his passion for art, creativity, and innovation. In that spirit, it is hoped that the Library will also become a place for future thinking about the ideas and philosophies that infused his life.

Walt Disney once said, "Somehow, I can't believe there are many heights that can't be scaled by a man who knows the secret of making dreams come true. This special secret, it seems to me, can be summarized in four C's. They are *Curiosity*, *Confidence*, *Courage*, and *Constancy*, and the greatest of these is *Confidence*. When you believe a thing, believe it all over, implicitly and unquestioningly." His family's commitment to the library project is a splendid example of this philosophy. It hasn't been easy having the courage to dream big. Diane allows, "My own ambitions were very modest at first. Walter, though constantly supportive, always urged that we had to do 'more.' Frankly, it is my dad's example that reassures me that we haven't wasted any of the Foundation's resources in our timid beginning, because everything we've done has led to a step forward rather than backward." Walter admits, "The greatest obstacle for me was having the mind-set to take on a project of this scope. The responsibility to do a great man justice with a library that bears his name is an awesome task. Walt Disney casts a giant shadow; he is known throughout the world, admired by many, and we are now responsible for making this the best tribute to the man, the men and women, the public that we possibly can. If this project is not successful, the Walt Disney Family is responsible."

New technologies and innovations will always be a part of the Library. The online museum will be a companion to the physical site, to allow those who can't visit the Library personally to do so virtually. The Web site may also offer a means for downloading information gathered during a Library visit. As for the future of the Walt Disney Family Library itself, Walter Miller has very clear goals: "I hope that it grows into a world class library that does the mission justice, to promote and discuss the life and times of Walt Disney. I hope that we can continue to support the collection of artifacts and memorabilia and continue to add to it. I want this to be a public space that will enrich the lives of many."

Cars

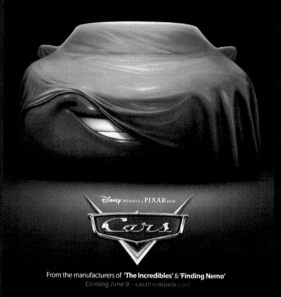

by Leslie Iwerks

DISNEY PRESENTS A PIXAR FILM

Cars

From the manufacturers of **'The Incredibles'** & **'Finding Nemo'**
Coming June 9 · carsthemovie.com

Since the formation of Pixar Animation Studios in 1986, audiences around the world have marveled at the combination of heartfelt storytelling and cutting-edge technology that makes their films so unique.

As Pixar celebrates its twenty-year anniversary in 2006 (with the release of their much-anticipated sixth feature film, *Cars*, in June), several Pixar creative leaders recently spent some time reflecting on the creative culture in their state-of-the-art animation studio in Emeryville, California.

"I think that [founders] Steve [Jobs] and John [Lasseter] and Ed [Catmull] are just smart to sort of let us just do what we do," says *Finding Nemo* director Andrew Stanton. "We really get a lot of creative freedom here, more than I've ever seen or heard about ever. And the other thing is that if it's not good enough, always do it again, even if it's the eleventh hour. The minute we start making choices—or movies—by second-guessing what we think people want to see, I think will be the day we start going on the decline. Everything has been, 'What do we want to see?'"

"I think if [a director] is personally invested in an idea, they're going to be able to hang with it through all those endless meetings and all the time it takes to make these films," notes *The Incredibles* director Brad Bird. "It's a tremendous benefit to have a personal stake in it. Even though they're big and there is a 'Pixar feel' to all of these films, I think they feel personal, and the reason people connect with them is because of that."

In 1999, after the demanding production process of *Toy Story 2*, director John Lasseter set off on a two-month-long cross country journey with his wife and five sons. Out on the open road with no preset plans except to "dip their feet into the Atlantic," John and family experienced the roadside America very few are able to see. As they drove pass the growing number of strip malls, chain stores, and fast-food restaurants, they found themselves veering off onto the "roads less traveled" to soak in the sights, sounds, and down-home cooking that are native only to the less prominent areas of the country.

John's passions and hobbies have been many over the years, but as he has said himself, "Slice open one of my veins and cartoons will pour out, and then open another vein and you'll get a flood of motor oil." Paul Lasseter, John's father, worked as a parts manager at a Chevrolet dealership when John was growing up, and the memories of everything *cars* made a lasting impression. His lifelong passion for the automobile took on a new form when he announced upon return from vacation that his next feature film would be about cars. Just as he and his family did, these car characters would also experience life, in all its manifestations, out on the open road.

The ensuing years of development catapulted John and his production team into the throes of the racing world. For the many Pixar car lovers, the research phase of the project was a dream come true. They journeyed to racetracks far and wide, met the legends of the racing community, and experienced firsthand the exhilarating thrill of whipping race cars around turns at speeds up to 200 miles per hour. John, the animators, and the story department embarked on their own field trip down the byways of Route 66. Here they experienced the stories, characters, and richness of towns that had fallen by the wayside to the four-lane superhighways of the modern United States. The team spared no expense in taking in life to the fullest—a characteristic experience if John Lasseter is at the helm. "John tries to

BELOW: John Lasseter, the creative leader at Pixar and director of such animated classics as *Toy Story*, *A Bug's Life*, and now, *Cars*.

have a good time with everybody and everything, and he's all about living life big," notes *Monsters, Inc.*, director Pete Docter. "Everything and anything he's inspired by." Who they met, what they saw, and how they felt would become the genesis of a new story, with characters as compelling as any Pixar has ever created.

The story team, headed by the late story genius, Joe Ranft, began the long process of shaping a massive story puzzle while developing the memorable characters inspired from their travels. "I love characters, I like people," mused Ranft. "I'm very curious about what makes people tick. And then you get these characters that are not real, but it's an illusion that they are alive and they've got something inside them that's motivating them and driving them. I love trying to figure out people, even if they're a bug or a toy or a car or a fish. On some level, they're people."

To animate cars with facial expression and body exaggeration is no simple feat. The development team scoured every book, documentary, film, and article that chronicled the history of Route 66, the history of cars, and the urbanization of the American West. Inspirational storyboards, paintings, and concepts lined the halls of Pixar. The animators were motivated by the successful 1952 Disney animated short, "Susie the Little Blue Coupe," which infused a charming personality to a little blue coupe going through life's trials and tribulations. Just as the Disney animators had experienced, the Pixar animators were challenged with the feat of bringing personality and practical motivation to a car. In this case, their characters ranged from an elderly 1920s Tin Lizzy up through the snappy race cars of today.

"You're searching for the emotion of the scene," Joe Ranft explained. "You're searching for the story you want to tell. And then, 'okay, that's what we want to say, but what's the best way to say it? What's the most elegant way to say it? What's the simplest way to say it?' And I believe it's not just the storyboard people, it's the editors as well. That's what John's so great at as a director, as his [discovery of] 'That's it! That's the story we're telling and that's the feeling we want!' Every other department is then on board to use the environment, the color, the lighting, the animation, to unify, to really make the strongest possible statement."

Since his Academy Award–winning days of lamps come to life in "Luxo Jr.," and the now-beloved cast of playthings in *Toy Story* and *Toy Story 2*, John has consistently infused warmth, humor, and heartfelt emotion into normally inanimate objects. His methods for animating the lamps in "Luxo Jr." continue two decades later in creating car characters. "One of the things about character animation is giving a personality to an object through movement, and I've always loved bringing inanimate objects to life," notes Lasseter. "Just through pure movement, you give it complete life and personality. I get thinking about the object and maintaining the integrity of the object and pull personality and movement and physics out of that. One of the things that is so important to me in the films that we make here is the heart, is the emotion. Walt Disney always said, 'for every laugh, there should be a tear, and for every tear, there should be a laugh.' The heart of a film is what stays with an audience long after they've seen the film."

In keeping with Pixar's previous five films, *Cars* captures the heart (or change of heart) in lead character Lightning McQueen (Owen Wilson), as he is unexpectedly forced off the fast lane of racing success to experience the simple life in the retired Route 66 town of Radiator Springs. Separated from his driver en route to the California Piston Cup championship, McQueen accidentally wreaks havoc upon the town's old Route 66 road. When the town mayor, Doc Hudson (Paul Newman) demands that he redeem himself and repave the roads, he is kept "in the pit" for days beyond his will.

McQueen's unrelenting quest for racing success is suddenly challenged by the town's offbeat characters, who, unlike McQueen, have not been swept away the facade of fame and sponsorship. McQueen sees firsthand the impact that "progress" has made on the now-decaying towns of Route 66. The inhabitants of Radiator Springs (voiced by Bonnie Hunt, Larry the Cable Guy, and legendary race car champion Richard Petty) enjoy life for the simple pleasures, making do with what they have, while appreciating the glory days of old. As Lightning McQueen is forced to sit and live in the "now," he must hold on for an even greater ride.

The richness and beauty of the American West has been handcrafted by the master concept artists, animators, technicians, and lighting designers Pixar has cultivated over the years. From their earliest developments of particle systems, motion blur, self-shadowing, depth of field and texturing which were breakthrough achievements in such Pixar shorts as "Andre & Wally B," "Luxo Jr.," and "Tin Toy," it is no surprise that they continue to push the CG medium into unprecedented terrain.

The technical department headed by Eben Ostby takes computer animation directly behind the wheels to experience the texture of the gravel, the heat of the pavement, and the exhaust of the engines as the muscle cars scream around the racetrack bends. Ostby recalls the "old" days (the early 1980s), when "thousands of trees on a hillside got pretty exciting." Today, Pixar delivers breathtaking panoramas of the American landscape, from dramatic waterfalls to the redwood forest and the red rock mountains, to the vast terrain of the desert and the dilapidated

and flashy automobiles of the 1950s. "John always pushes us to do something new," notes Ostby. "We're way beyond the days when the story dictated the medium because now you can find a way to reflect anything written."

The drive for authenticity of environment and character has been the overarching influence of John Lasseter. "I've always been inspired by my limitations," explains Lasseter. "Art challenges technology, and technology inspires art."

Veteran producer Darla Anderson oversees all aspects of the animation process, monitoring every nuance of the budget to keep the show running on schedule. Having produced *A Bug's Life*, *Monsters, Inc.*, and now *Cars*, Darla is familiar with the myriad challenges associated with her team's innate need to stretch beyond their means. "Never is there one ounce of 'Yeah, yeah, we've done this before,'" Darla muses. "Making great stories with great characters is hard, and everyone has a healthy respect for that."

Pixar's feature films have historically been built upon driving action scenes, nonstop plot twists, and outlandishly funny characters. The uniqueness of *Cars* is that it equally contrasts the loud, thumping energy of the racetrack, with the refreshingly quiet, tranquil pace of Radiator Springs. Here, we are allowed to ruminate in the gentle moments of life that often go unseen and unappreciated, a story task sometimes more difficult to achieve than it may seem.

"Every film has its own different challenges," notes Joe Ranft. "You can exaggerate—for example, in a caricature you're making everything bigger, making everything louder. But you can also exaggerate by making them softer. One of the things I've learned is the tricks that worked on the last movie don't necessarily work on this movie. And you sit there with it. And you spend a lot of time with a sort of uncertainty trying to find what this particular film should be, you know, that's *different*."

Different is what the Pixar team has again achieved. In June of 2006, *Cars* rolls out to theaters across the country. For those who have had the pleasure to work with director John Lasseter, he is known as the man who brings out the child in everyone. As a result, *Cars* brings out the child in all of us, and reminds us that life isn't all about the reward, but the journey, and in this case—the journey *is* the destination. ♥

Go to

www.Disney.com/DisneyInsider

Animation Generation:
ACROSS THE DECADES WITH BAMBI

by Charles Solomon

The last of the "Big Five" features that set the standard by which all animated films are still judged, *Bambi* represented the culmination of more than a decade of training and experimentation. Walt Disney asked his artists to meld the warmth of *Snow White and the Seven Dwarfs*, the refined character animation of *Pinocchio*, the charm of *Dumbo*, the polished draftsmanship of *Fantasia*, and the visual imagination of the "Silly Symphonies" into the story of a young deer's coming of age. The effort required nearly six years, but the result was a lyrical vision of nature that has never been equaled.

"*Bambi* was such a breakthrough! If you compare the deer and the rabbits in *Bambi* to the ones in *Snow White*, you can see how much the artists had grown in terms of knowing the anatomy of the animals, how to move them, and how to make personalities out of them," says animator Andreas Deja. "When you look at the realism in *Bambi*, you almost think it shouldn't work—it's *so* realistic. Milt Kahl said that there's nothing wrong with realism, but there are problems with the way people handle it. He meant you have to know the anatomy of the animal, then take that knowledge and interpret it."

Sidney Franklin, the director of *The Barretts of Wimpole Street*, *Private Lives*, and *The Good Earth*, bought the film rights to Felix Salten's best seller, *Bambi*, in 1933. After two years of experiments and tests, he realized it would be impossible to film the book in live action, so he approached Disney about animating it. The story excited Walt, who originally hoped to release it for Christmas of 1938. Neither he nor his artists realized the film would present such enormous challenges.

In early 1937, Walt chose Perce Pearce and Larry Morey to head up the story development crew. The Studio was busier than it had ever been: *Snow White* was nearing completion; at the same time, crews were working on *Pinocchio*, several Mickey Mouse cartoons, and the last "Silly Symphonies." The staff had long outgrown the Studio buildings on Hyperion Avenue in the Silver Lake district of Los Angeles: artists were crowded chockablock in small rooms; others worked in nearby offices, apartments, and bungalows.

Walt set Pearce, Morey, and a small crew to work in offices on Seward Street in Hollywood. Except for occasional meetings with Walt and Franklin, who continued as an adviser, the *Bambi* crew was left to its own devices.

THESE PAGES: The delicate pastels of artist Ty Wong brought a visual poetry to *Bambi*. "The influence Ty had on this film made the film!" said legendary Disney artist Marc Davis, one of *Bambi*'s main designers and animators.

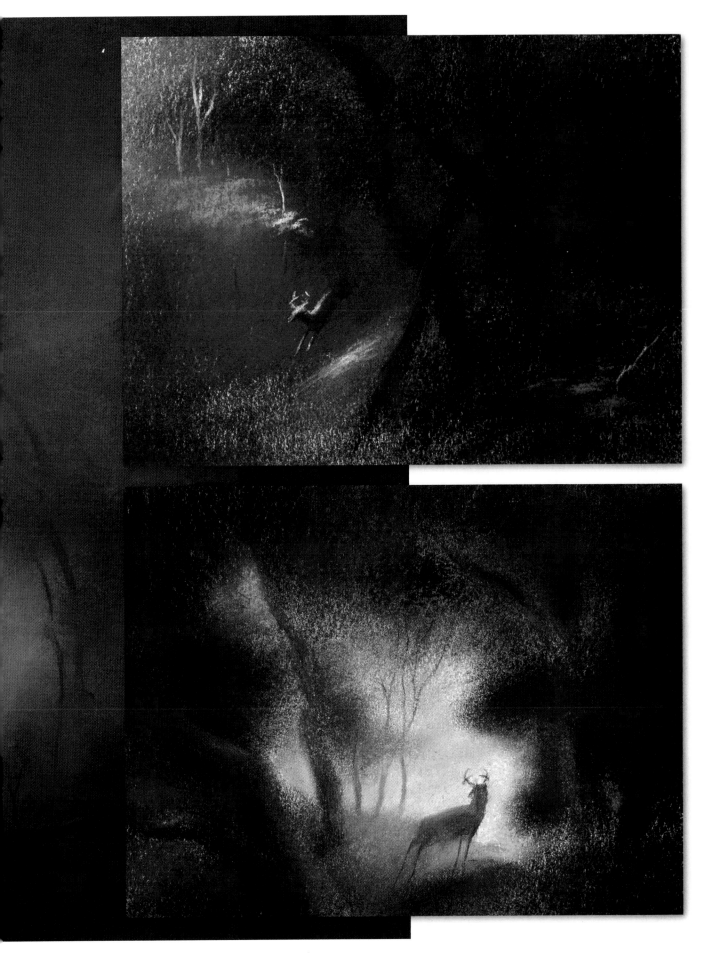

Disney Legend Marc Davis, who began doing story and character development as soon as he finished animating on *Snow White*, recalled, "I don't think Walt dropped in more than two or three times all the time we were on Seward Street. He would leave you alone for a long time if he thought you were developing something that was all right or if he didn't have any ideas on it. But we were the first group to move into the new studio in Burbank. We finished the story in the 3-B wing, and he was in and out of there regularly. Whenever Perce would announce, 'Man is in the forest!' it meant Walt was down the hall."

While the story was taking shape, the animators studied the anatomy and movements of deer, rabbits, skunks, and other animals who would appear in the film. For *Bambi* to be believable on the screen, the animal characters would have to be much more realistic than anything the Studio had attempted previously. The realism Deja praises required exceptional draftsmanship and a thorough knowledge of animal anatomy and motion.

Walt had begun underwriting an ambitious training program for his artists in 1932. Under Don Graham, a noted drawing instructor from the Chouinard Art Institute in Los Angeles, the program included life drawing, acting, anatomy, and action analysis. One of the lecturers was the artist Rico Lebrun, who was known for his studies of animals. Animator Frank Thomas recalled that Lebrun obtained the carcass of a fawn from the forestry service during the preparations for *Bambi*. He spent a week dissecting the animal and explaining its underlying musculature—ignoring its worsening stench—while the animators held their breaths and tried to concentrate on their drawings.

But the main instructor for the *Bambi* artists was Bernard Garbutt. As Frank Thomas and Ollie Johnston wrote, "'Garby' was the animal expert: he could draw any animal, at any age, in any position, and he set the standard for everyone else to follow." To supplement his lectures, Garbutt led drawing sessions, organized trips to the zoo, and brought in live animals to serve as models. Garbutt's delicate pencil sketches captured the anatomy and movements of a deer, but they lacked the fluidity needed for lifelike animation. They also failed to suggest the personality a character would need to entertain an audience.

As a student, Marc Davis spent his days sketching the animals in the Fleishhacker Zoo in San Francisco; in the evenings, he studied animal anatomy in the public library. He hoped to capture movement in fine art, in the tradition of Frederick Remington's bronze sculptures. Because he could already draw deer accurately, Davis was able to concentrate on making them "animatable" and giving them personalities. He studied the facial expressions of human babies and transferred their characteristics to deer, rabbits, and skunks. When Walt saw Davis's sketches, he said, "I want to see these drawings on the screen."

Johnston and Thomas wrote, "(Marc's) deer looked like

deer, for they had lost none of their essential animal appearance or character, but they could be understood as having human thoughts and feelings. Faline was coy, she was spirited and playful, she had a twinkle in her eye; she sparkled."

In addition to Davis, four other animators from the group Walt would later dub the "Nine Old Men" made important contributions to *Bambi*: Milt Kahl, Ollie Johnston, Frank Thomas, and Eric Larson.

"On *Pinocchio*, Walt realized what kind of an artist Milt was and had him design most of the characters for his features," says Deja. "Milt would base the model sheets on story sketches

and other artists' work—for *Bambi*, it was mainly Marc's drawings—and he would give them a final look that was very appealing and animatable. But his draftsmanship was so elevated, it was sometimes difficult for the other animators to follow."

Deja also praises Kahl's animation of the adolescent Bambi, which presented special challenges. Bambi is no longer a wobbly, charming child. As he's grown, he's become more dignified and self-assured, subtle qualities that are difficult to communicate in animation. "When Man is approaching and Bambi can't find Faline, Milt animated these beautiful leaps interspersed with pauses. Bambi can't see her, and Milt communicates a slight feeling of panic before the character leaps out of the scene—it's just stunning work."

At a screening of the restored *Bambi* in 2005, viewers were struck by Ollie Johnston's understated animation of Bambi meeting the Great Prince of the Forest. Seeing the respect with which the other deer greet the Prince, Bambi looks up eagerly. When the stag regards him coolly, the fawn drops his head, lowers his ears, and swallows, uncertain what to do.

OPPOSITE: Walt arranged for two live deer—appropriately named Bambi and Faline—to live at the Studio so his animators could study the animals as they grew.

TOP, LEFT: Animator Eric Larson brought a touch of his own wisdom to the character of wise old Friend Owl.

TOP, RIGHT: Affectionately known as "Garby," artist Bernard Garbutt was the *Bambi* animal expert, and regularly organized trips to the Los Angeles Zoo, as in this visit with animator Retta Scott.

CENTER: Art director Tom Codrick recognized the revolutionary influence that Ty Wong's almost-mystical pastels could have on *Bambi* and attempted to adapt the lyrical touch suggested by Ty's works into the film's backgrounds and overall style.

LEFT: A Western landscape painter tries to reproduce the physical details, a Chinese artist strives to capture sensations. In *Bambi*, artist Tyrus Wong made a character out of the settings.

ABOVE: Thumper takes Bambi skating on a frozen pond, as animated by the legendary Frank Thomas.

ABOVE: During the course of his career, veteran Disney animator Andreas Deja has often found inspiration in the work of many of his talented predecessors, who brought *Bambi* to life.

"It's one of those scenes that's so subtle, you think it couldn't be done in animation," comments Deja. "When you want to show a change, you have to make it graphically clear, and Bambi is going through such a subtle mood shift. Ollie Johnston handled it with the tact and sensitivity he always brought to his animation."

Johnston replied, "I believed all my characters were alive; they were doing what they wanted to do, or hoped to do. I couldn't think of them any other way. They live and breathe in my life, and I feel like I'm part of them."

When he animated Scar in *The Lion King*, Deja looked at Johnston's work in *Bambi* for clues on how to balance the conflicting demands of keeping an animal realistic and making him a vivid character. "Because Scar was a villain and enjoyed being a villain, he had a different range than the *Bambi* characters: with villains usually you can go further and get into the emotions a little more," he explains.

"There are scenes where Scar will lift a paw and flick it: I had to make sure that paw didn't become a hand. There are examples in *Bambi* that tell you how far you should go. In one scene of Ollie's near the beginning of the film, Faline chases Bambi around a little pond that he falls into. Bambi has had it, so he uses his wrist to wipe some water off his muzzle. It's really a humanized action, but it's handled very carefully, so it still reads like a gesture that a particular deer could make."

Frank Thomas animated what must rank as the most famous sequence in the film: the first winter, when Thumper and

Bambi explore a frozen pond. "The water's stiff," Thumper announces, batting the ice with his foot. It's a delightful moment that illustrates Walt's insistence on humor that grows out of the characters' reactions to their environment, not gags writers put in their mouths.

"It's a very animatable piece of story work because of the contrasts in the characters," Deja explains. "Thumper wants to show Bambi how much fun he can have on the ice, but Thumper is basically a champion ice skater. Bambi can't cope with the ice on his long, stiff legs, and he falls. Bambi does awkward things that a deer can't really do, like getting his back legs crossed and almost tied in a knot, but it looks so believable. Thumper unwinds his legs and turns him all around—it's an animator's dream to animate this kind of material, and no one else could have brought that sequence to life the way Frank did."

In this sequence, as in many others, Thumper nearly steals the film. Much of his charm comes from Peter Behn's lively, unaffected vocal performance. "I think all the animators—Ollie, Frank, and Milt—really enjoyed the character," Deja continues. "His design is a little looser and rounder, so they could go a little further with him than with the deer. He's also very self-assured when he takes on the role of Bambi's self-appointed teacher. The exuberance and the enthusiasm in his voice brought so much to the film. You can get voices that are clowny and 'actor-y,' but these characters sound like a bunch of kids going through these situations. They're real."

Eric Larson was in his early thirties when he animated the Owl in *Bambi*. The character suggests a genial, somewhat impatient older man. He knows the ways of the forest, and explains the changing seasons to Bambi, Thumper, and Flower. But he still gets fed up with the "twitterpated" birds whose chatter disturbs his sleep.

When Andreas Deja met him in the 1970s, Eric Larson was in charge of training a new generation of Disney animators. Deja discovered the old artist had come to resemble his character. "It went beyond the appearance to his personality," Deja recalls. "Eric was wise. He tried to communicate the Disney philosophy to us, not just how to animate something, but what Disney animation means, what you need to think about before you animate and what Walt tried to achieve in his work. There was a sort of an owl wisdom to Eric."

One of the most important characters in *Bambi* has no voice and doesn't really move. The forest isn't just a backdrop for the animated actors, it's an essential component of the story. The Disney artists moved Salten's story from the Black Forest of Germany to the woods of eastern North America, and sent photographer Maurice Day to Maine, where he shot thousands of feet of reference film. But the look of *Bambi* was largely the creation of the Chinese artist Tyrus Wong. Deja says, "Tyrus made a character out of the forest. It can be a scary character during the winter storm or a pleasant one in the spring. But if you look at the backgrounds, even without the characters in them, they convey so much feeling and emotion."

"I'd get the script, and it might say, 'early morning: the deer go out on the meadow,'" Wong recalls. "I would try to create the atmosphere of a meadow on a foggy morning; it was the mood they wanted me to capture."

Working primarily in watercolor and gouache, Wong made hundreds of small, exquisite sketches that suggested the beauties of the forest at various times of day and in different seasons. A Western landscape painter tries to reproduce the physical details of a specific location; a Chinese artist strives to capture the sensations a scene evokes. Wong's paintings suggest the forest the viewer experiences within himself, rather than the forest he sees.

"My paintings were always very poetic, and that's from the Chinese tradition that a poet is a painter and a painter is a poet," explains Wong. "The aim isn't to be realistic, like a Western painting; it's not like a photograph. It's the feeling you're trying to get: in a sense, it is real and yet it isn't real."

"Each of the so-called Disney classics has a style of its own, not just one style with different characters moving through it, and the style of *Bambi* is Tyrus's," said Davis, who had been friends with Wong since they met in art school in the early 1930s. "His work always had a magic to it: an oak leaf is an oak leaf, but it's a different oak leaf when he gets through with it. You perceive it differently and appreciate the way he evokes all oak leaves."

Bambi was not a hit when it released in 1942. "For somewhat different reasons, both *Bambi* and *Fantasia*, were highly unsuccessful when they came out," says Roy E. Disney. "*Fantasia* was ahead of its time. *Bambi* was a sweet little story about 'please don't kill the deer,' when we were talking about killing human beings, and it just didn't sell."

Over the decades, audiences and critics have come to recognize what a singular achievement *Bambi* was. The Disney artists took great pride in their work on one of Walt's most extraordinary visions. Johnston and Thomas noted, "Of all the great pictures Walt Disney made, this was his favorite. It is ours, too."

Deja found the standard those artists set rather daunting when he began work on *Bambi and the Great Prince of the Forest* sixty years later. "When I looked at the old model sheets, I thought, 'Oh boy—I'm in trouble!' You look at these fantastically beautiful drawings and realize you have to hook up with them. I really enjoyed doing my first scenes of *Bambi*: I wanted it to feel like a deer and to feel like the first *Bambi*, but not look like a copy of *Bambi*. There's a real sense of satisfaction in realizing, 'Yes, I can tackle something like this now.'"

Disney
Bambi II

Bambi II takes place during an untold but critical chapter in the life of young Bambi. Bambi knows his mother is gone. His stoic father, the Great Prince of the Forest, has little choice but to raise Bambi on his own. He has no experience caring for a fawn, but as wise Friend Owl suggests, who better to raise the young prince than the Great Prince himself?

Bambi learns valuable life lessons and the ways of the forest as a new season begins. But there are many adventures and obstacles that both Bambi and the Great Prince must overcome together as they realize they have much to teach each other. Together, they can look forward to a bright future.

Disney World

Come to a Party

Go away!! Burny is busy

Disney Goes Wide

The Story of Lady and the Tramp

by Paula Sigman Lowery

With the success of *Cinderella* and the two animated features that followed, *Alice in Wonderland* and *Peter Pan*, it might have seemed as though the future of animation at the Walt Disney Studio was guaranteed. But it was *Lady and the Tramp*—Walt Disney's first wide-screen animated feature—that played the crucial role in assuring the continuation of Disney animation. It also saved the life of a dog.

The story of *Lady and the Tramp*, however, began long before the film lit theater screens in 1955. It was back in 1937—just before the release of Disney's first full-length animated feature, *Snow White and the Seven Dwarfs*—that Lady got her start. Walt Disney was visiting one of his key character artists and writer, Joe Grant, and his wife, Jennie. Joe had given Jennie a springer spaniel the previous Christmas, whom they called Lady. Jennie adored Lady. According to Joe's daughter Carol, when Walt saw the dog, with her fur fluffed out around her rump, wiggling like a flirty little skirt as she walked, he said, "Joe, why don't you work up a story about Lady."

Disney registered the title "Lady" for a short cartoon in November 1937, and Joe started his story work the next month, drawing a series of charming illustrations of his pet at play. With the success of *Snow White*, Walt turned to his next full-length features, *Pinocchio* and *Fantasia*, and Joe took on new responsibilities as founder and head of Disney's new Character Model Department. Lady remained at home, where she continued to enjoy Joe and Jennie's undivided attention . . . until the birth of their daughter, Carol.

Lady's confusion at the change in her status renewed Joe's interest in his dog story. From July through October 1939, he worked with key Disney story men Ted Sears, Bill Cottrell, and Jack Miller on a new outline which featured a story told entirely in dialogue and from Lady's point of view. In this version, the already-grown Lady lives in a house with Mr. and Mrs. Fred, and Major, a cat of which she does not approve, believing cats "are not nice." In general, she is quite content with her life, although she does not like her neighbors very well, noting, "They have two children who are named Stop It Bertram and Come Here Warren."

The neighbor children eventually disappeared, but other elements from this early treatment are surprisingly familiar. According to Lady, "Mrs. Fred came back with a baby and a mean old nurse who said I was a dirty animal and made me feel bad. I was kept away from the baby and even locked on the inside of the porch. I felt even worse when Mr. Fred didn't understand and thought I was jealous of the baby." The arrogant cat, however, can go in and out as he pleases, and cozies up to the nurse in order to be petted and fed. Lady feels sorry for herself, and decides to run away. She wants to see the baby before she goes, and slips up to the nursery, where she discovers a rat about to attack the baby. Lady rushes to the rescue and dispatches the rat, but in doing so she accidentally tips over the baby basket. Mr. and Mrs. Fred think she has tried to hurt the baby, and throw her out of the house, where she huddles forlornly in the rain. They find the rat, all is forgiven, and the story ends at Christmastime, with Lady herself a mother to five puppies.

The story had drama and personality, but it still wasn't right—even for a short cartoon. Walt knew it needed

...and *NOW* his Happiest Motion Picture!

Walt Disney's
Lady
AND THE
Tramp

COLOR BY
TECHNICOLOR

WITH THE HAPPIEST SONGS OF ALL!
HE'S A TRAMP • BELLA NOTTE
THE SIAMESE CAT SONG
LA LA LU • PEACE ON EARTH

the FIRST all-cartoon feature in
CINEMASCOPE

From the novel by
Ward Greene

Distributed by Buena Vista Film Distribution Co., Inc. COPYRIGHT WALT DISNEY PRODUCTIONS

something more. In September 1940, with *Pinocchio* released and *Fantasia* nearly done, he teamed Joe up with director and animator Dick Huemer. They introduced a mother-in-law, turned Major into twin Siamese cats named Nip and Tuck, and created a pair of rivals for Lady's affection: Boris, an aristocratic Russian wolfhound, and Homer, a mongrel. Over the next few months Studio story men Walt Pfeiffer, Berk Anthony, Dunbar Roman, Bill Jones, and Frank Tashlin contributed ideas. In 1941, Walt began thinking of the "Lady" project as a feature, rather than a short. By this time, the story started with Lady as a puppy, and Homer had become "Bozo." Ted Sears returned to the project and increased the drama with sequences in which Lady is muzzled; locked in the cellar, where she has a horrible nightmare; is banished in error; and finally, is picked up by a dogcatcher and taken to the pound, where she faces death in the gas chamber until reprieved at the last minute by the family. Once again the story ends happily at Christmastime, with Lady and her swain, now called "Rags," and their new family.

Story refinement continued throughout 1941. Then came December 7, a day that changed everything for the United States—and certainly for the Studio. Following the attack on Pearl Harbor, the U.S. entered World War II and the U.S. military moved onto the Disney studio lot. Overnight production shifted to military training films and other patriotic efforts that continued throughout the war years, leaving little time for story development. It would be two more years before Lady met her Tramp.

In 1943, Ward Greene, the general manager for King Features Syndicate (the group that published the Disney comics) sent Roy O. Disney several stories he had written for *Cosmopolitan* magazine. Ward thought they might make good cartoons. Roy passed the stories along to Walt. One of them was "Happy Dan, the Whistling Dog." Walt saw a trait in Ward's dog that could "plus" the Homer/Rags/Bozo character, and give him more personality. Happy Dan wasn't just "happy-go-lucky"; he was a cynic, and had figured out an angle to being "man's best friend." Although he had a home, he made regular visits to different families, who called him by different names, and gave him plenty to eat. Walt asked Ward to come

up with a way to bring the dogs together, and the result was "Happy Dan, the Whistling Dog, and Miss Patsy, the Beautiful Spaniel." As Disney archivist Dave Smith observes, "For years, Walt had enjoyed pitting different story people against each other, figuring that out of his competition he could get the best story. In this case, it worked again. The story men, who had been working on the project, got the incentive to make an extra push on their vision."

Walt was now convinced the story of *Lady and the Tramp* was more suited for a feature-length film than a short cartoon. But development of *Lady*, like that for *Alice in Wonderland* and *Peter Pan*, took a backseat to the continuing war work, which provided Walt with the means to keep his Studio operating.

After the war, Walt struggled to return the Studio to full production. He began experimenting with live-action films that included animated sequences, and combined short cartoons with a common theme of popular music into feature-length "packages" pictures. For his first post-war full-length single-story animated film, he turned once more to a traditional, beloved fairy tale. *Cinderella*, released in 1950, was a huge success, and the future of feature animation at Disney seemed assured.

But the next film caused Walt to worry. *Alice in Wonderland* (1951) was based on a well-known British story, and critics and audiences alike—particularly English audiences—felt Disney's version didn't capture the whimsical spirit of Lewis Carroll's classic. Costs were skyrocketing as well, and with the hugely complicated *Sleeping Beauty* in development, Walt had concerns that the Studio could sustain continued animation production.

Walt saw *Lady and the Tramp* as a chance to rebuild and renew his artists' creative spirit. An original story would give them an opportunity to hone their storytelling and animation skills without having to deal with an audience's preconceptions. Walt also thought it would be a more economic production, without the complications that arose in animating human characters. Even the characters' "wardrobe" was expensive, since to seem real, the clothing—or drapery—had to have movement of its own.

Walt expected that *Lady and the Tramp* would cost about $1 million, in comparison to *Peter Pan*, which he anticipated would cost $3 million. Work on *Lady and the Tramp* would give the Studio a much needed breather. In a 1952 story meeting on *Lady and the Tramp*, Walt said, "I have confidence that if we get going on this, we're liable to get a picture out of here that will be a change of pace in many ways. A thing like this in the plant will be a relief, and I have no doubt about us being able to build a good story with it. A good many things we might have questioned a few years ago, we won't have any trouble with. It will all come out. Iron itself out as we roll through. In other words, we put one in that's not going to be the problem child that *Sleeping Beauty* is going to be."

OPPOSITE, TOP LEFT: *Lady and the Tramp* boasted the talents of seven of Walt Disney's legendary "Nine Old Men" of animation, including John Lounsbery. Here, John draws Tony, the emotional restaurateur, who sings the film's charmingly romantic ballad, "Belle Notte."

OPPOSITE, TOP RIGHT: Claude Coats and a team of background artists, including Al Dempster, Ralph Hulett, and Eyvind Earle, were responsible for painting the panoramic *Lady and the Tramp* backgrounds necessitated by the wide-screen CinemaScope process.

OPPOSITE, BOTTOM: Story artists Ed Penner and Joe Rinaldi pose with the live-action models of *Lady and Tramp*. Ed was responsible for finding the Tramp model, a stray who was actually a "she."

Animation began in early 1953, and Walt quickly realized it wasn't going to be as easy as he had expected. In their recent films, the animators had been drawing broad, cartoon-like animals. For *Lady and the Tramp* to work, the dogs needed to seem real. Directing animator Milt Kahl warned, "These things aren't easy to draw. It's going to be expensive, to get a good result." He continued, "I don't think it's quite as tough as *Peter Pan*. You don't have the tight characters, Peter and Wendy, to do, but it's a problem. Guys aren't used to drawing and animating these things to look fairly real."

Walt urged his artists to do their best to keep costs down. "If we can't," he worried, "I hate to think of the future of the business. Because things can only stand so much." But he believed the animators could "get into the feel of these

torch singer Peggy Lee and composer Sonny Burke had written several songs to move the story along, including the showstopping "He's a Tramp," sung by the sultry ex-star of the dog-and-pony follies, Peg.

But before the year was out, *Lady and the Tramp* faced a new complication: wide-screen. The 1950s had brought a threat to the motion picture industry in the form of television. Faced with the possibility of losing their audience to the small screen, the movie studios needed to find a way in which television could not compete. They turned to technology, to make the motion picture experience bigger and more spectacular than ever before.

The first wide-screen format, introduced in 1952, was Cinerama. It was spectacular, but not terribly practical. It

characters," they would move ahead smoothly and efficiently.

The Studio brought in a group of dogs for the animators to study. They filmed the dog that modeled for Tramp doing trots, walks, and turns, and studied footage of dogs eating, drinking, and scratching. This additional study added costs to the film, but it enabled the animators to achieve the real dog action that Walt wanted. It also turned out to be just as complicated to draw the dogs' fur as it would have been to handle the movement of human characters and their clothing. In spite of the Studio's economies, *Lady and the Tramp* was now estimated to cost $3 million. No longer was it a "low-budget" film.

At last, the story issues were resolving nicely. Famed

used three individual 35mm cameras positioned so that when the three images were projected (onto a large, curved screen), they merged to present a single, nearly seamless, wide-screen image. It was cumbersome to shoot and costly to project, and there were only a few theaters in the country equipped to present Cinerama films.

The real breakthrough was the development of CinemaScope, which used a special anamorphic lens fitted onto an ordinary camera. The lens enabled filmmakers to take a wide-screen setup and "squeeze" it into the square shape of regular 35mm film frames. Anamorphic lenses attached to projects would "unsqueeze" the image, and present the original wide-screen shot envisioned by the filmmaker. Eager as always to push the envelope, Walt immediately saw that wide screen could offer a new challenge to his animators, and a new experience for his audiences. In spite of the added expense, *Lady and the Tramp* would be his first CinemaScope feature.

For many studios, only the most important films merited a CinemaScope treatment, and because not all theaters were equipped to handle wide-screen projection, some films actually were shot twice—once with standard lenses, and once with the special anamorphic lenses. That's exactly what happened with *Lady and the Tramp*. Walt couldn't afford a limited release, so he produced two completely separate versions of the film. This was a special challenge for the layout artists, who had to stage the action so that it worked equally well for both the traditional framing and the wider stage af-

forded by the full background. The animators had to produce additional animation that carried the action to the edges of the stage. Walt explained, "Visually, CinemaScope gave us the opportunity—indeed, the necessity—to experiment with action, groupings, and setting. It made us re-examine many of our work habits. We were able, of course, to do more in our backgrounds and settings because we had a larger canvas on which to work."

It definitely made the production more complicated. Animator and director Woolie Reitherman, one of Walt's legendary "Nine Old Men," said, "We were forced to experiment with action, groupings, and setting. Models were built to the scale of one-and-a-half-inches to the foot and principle characters were cut out of celluloid and used to get the proper size

ABOVE: The panoramic CinemaScope frame enabled the layout and background artists to fully explore the charming early-twentieth-century locales. The resulting "wide vistas" provided a lush stage for Lady and the rest of the animated cast.

RIGHT: The wide-screen vistas brought new levels of excitement to the animated world of *Lady and the Tramp*.

131

ABOVE: Singer and actress Peggy Lee provided the vocals for (and co-wrote) the song "He's a Tramp." Miss Lee and co-author Sonny Burke also contributed "The Siamese Cat Song."

THESE PAGES: The wonderful wide-screen world of *Lady and the Tramp*.

and positioning relationship with backgrounds. These helped us solve the problem of perspective on the wide screen." In an article for *Films in Review*, Oscar-winning animator Ward Kimball noted that one of the animators' greatest discoveries was that in CinemaScope, "cartoon characters move, not the backgrounds. Because there is more space, the characters can move about without getting outside the visual angle." They no longer performed "in one spot against a moving background," but could be moved through the scenes. They could also move in relation to each other." More characters could be shown simultaneously, with fewer separate cuts and separate scenes, "since the action takes place in continuous, unbroken movement across one wide vista." It was exciting and re-invigorating to the entire creative team. It also turned out to be far more expensive than Walt's original estimate. CinemaScope increased the film's cost by 30 percent; by the time *Lady and the Tramp* was released, it cost not one but *four* million dollars.

Walt Disney was delighted with the final film. He relished the freedom of telling an original story that didn't have to conform to an audience's preconceived notions—an issue with both *Alice in Wonderland* and *Peter Pan*. (He also took immense personal pleasure in having contributed the gag that introduced Lady; in the early days of his marriage he gave Lilly a chow puppy—in a hatbox—for Christmas.)

Audiences were equally delighted—so much so that *Lady and the Tramp* ended up as the top-grossing film for 1955. The success of *Lady and the Tramp* ensured the continued production of *Sleeping Beauty*, as well as the animated features that followed.

There's one more happy ending associated with the story of *Lady and the Tramp*. The character that gave the artists the most trouble was Tramp. Although Ward Greene's story work helped define his personality, the artists disagreed about his appearance. He needed to be a mongrel, tough enough to survive on the streets yet dashing enough to capture Lady's heart. One evening, story man Ed Penner saw a dog disappearing into the bushes. He was perfect for Tramp, but like Tramp, he was a stray, and Ed couldn't find him. Ed searched for several days before finally discovering the dog in the local pound, just hours away from being put down. Ed rescued him, and brought him to the Studio to serve as the artists' inspiration. "He" turned out to be a "she," and a puppy at that, but she still made a perfect Tramp. After she was filmed and studied, the dog—now called "Mitzie"—lived a life of ease, boarded at Studio expense. She was truly a "Cinderella" dog . . . but that's another story.

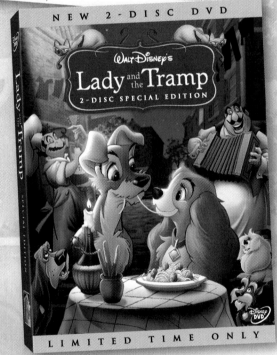

TOP: Ad art intended for theater owners to run in local newspapers makes sure to point out the wide-screen wonder of *Lady and the Tramp*. On the same bill: Walt Disney's *Switzerland*, the first People and Places short in CinemaScope.

ABOVE: *Lady and the Tramp* is unleashed on Disney DVD.

Curious...

The film's leading lady was modeled mainly by two cocker spaniels. One belonged to sequence director Ham Luske; the other, in a strange twist of fate, belonged to actress Verna Felton, who voiced the cat-loving, dog-hating Aunt Sarah.

The character of Peg was called "Mame" in the original script. When Dwight D. Eisenhower was elected president in 1952, the Studio worried about causing offense to the new First Lady, nicknamed "Mamie," and held a meeting to discuss changing the dog's name. Animator Frank Thomas recalled, "Everyone was thinking of chorus girls' names, theater names, and show people. Every so often [story man Ed] Penner would say, 'Why did Eisenhower have to get elected? "Mame" was the perfect name for this character.' For some reason, we were thinking of lower and lower types of females when Milt [Kahl] suddenly said, 'I've got it! Lil!' Walt looked at him with a pained expression and commented, 'That's *my* wife's name.' Milt came unglued and retired in confusion." Eventually the artists asked Mame's voice, Peggy Lee, if she would mind having the sultry showdog named after her. She consented graciously.

Toot, Whistle, Plunk and Boom *was Disney's first CinemaScope cartoon; released in December 1953, it won an Academy Award.*

The two-disc Special Platinum Edition DVD release of *Lady and the Tramp* features the CinemaScope version in an all-new digital restoration with enhanced picture and sound. Of particular interest are an early storyboard version of the film, never-before-seen abandoned and alternate sequences, and a new documentary on the making of the film.

Lost Disney

ADVENTURE THRU INNER SPACE

Presented by Monsanto

by Jeff Kurtti

"Monsanto's new Disneyland attraction, Adventure Thru Inner Space, takes visitors on a unique and exciting journey into the mysterious realm of the atom. The illusional journey begins when the inner space traveler climbs into his 'Atomobile' and enters the 'mighty microscope,' which is focused on a snowflake. He appears to shrink until the fragile snowflake becomes towering cliffs of ice. The trip continues and he becomes 'smaller and smaller' as he is exposed to scientific phenomena of crystalline structure and molecular composition."

—WED Enterprises (now Walt Disney Imagineering) Press Release, June 1967

In 1965, Walt Disney approached the Monsanto Company with the idea of building a new and expanded Tomorrowland at Disneyland. (The original Monsanto company, founded in 1901, was then a chemical concern with a focus on molecular research and new manmade materials.) The original Tomorrowland had, within a decade, become more of a "Todayland," and it was time to update the entire area, including replacing the Hall of Chemistry attraction (presented by Monsanto) with something that more enthusiastically depicted the excitement of the present and the expectations of the future.

The earliest concept for a ride into the world of the microscope actually appeared in 1957, as part of a proposed but never-built attraction called Adventures in Science. When the idea resurfaced in the 1960s for New Tomorrowland, Journey Into the Microscope (as it was originally called) was to take guests into the microscopic realm of a drop of water. The attraction was intended to share space with an exhibit to be presented by the Ford Motor Company.

The Ford attraction never materialized, and the design for Adventure Thru Inner Space (as it was renamed) was expanded to occupy the entire building. It was also decided that a snowflake would make a more exciting destination, and no doubt simpler to execute, than a drop of water.

Adventure Thru Inner Space opened as a free attraction with the debut of Disneyland's New Tomorrowland in June 1967.

One of the highlights of the attraction was the "mighty microscope," a thirty-seven-foot-long, twelve-foot-high microscope that appeared to "miniaturize" guests. Those waiting to board the chain of Omnimover "Atomobiles" for their microscopic mission could see other inner-space voyagers apparently shrinking as they moved through a transparent section of the microscope.

The concept for an adventure into the microscopic world grew from conversations between Walt Disney and Monsanto's Dr. Charles Allen Thomas about the public's interest in science. Although the exploration of outer space had received a great deal of publicity, Thomas felt it was research into "inner space" that was making the more tangible impact on people's daily lives. Many of the Imagineers who worked together on The Haunted Mansion came together to create this microscopic mission. Claude Coats designed the environments, with "Illusioneering" special effects created by Yale Gracey. The script was written by X. Atencio and narrated by Paul Frees. The theme song, "Miracles from Molecules," was composed by Academy Award–winning songwriters Richard M. Sherman and Robert B. Sherman, who also wrote "It's a Small World (After All)" and the score to *Mary Poppins*, among dozens of other popular tunes. Adventure Thru Inner Space was the premiere of the Disney-created Omnimover ride system, a rail-based "pod" vehicle that could control the speed, direction, and view of the visitor.

Because admission was free, young couples would board

Adventure
thru
Inner Space

PRESENTED BY MONSANTO

ABOVE: Adventure Thru Inner Space was constructed on the site of the Hall of Chemistry, a science-centered attraction sponsored by Monsanto that debuted during Disneyland Park's first year. The Hall offered stylish and futuristic displays of how "creative chemistry works for you."

BELOW: Postcards issued in the early years of Disneyland celebrate the Hall of Chemistry.

Disneyland *cordially invites you to be the guest of MONSANTO for an "Adventure Thru Inner Space" in Tomorrow-land. Children and Juniors not accompanied by an Adult must present this coupon to be admitted to the attraction.*

© 1966 Walt Disney Productions

F000001

TOP: Disneyland guests found themselves miniaturized deep inside a snowflake molecule.

CENTER LEFT: In addition to the "molecular miracles" of the attraction itself, Adventure Thru Inner Space offered a celebration of Monsanto technology.

CENTER RIGHT: A ticket designed to keep guests off the attraction—since the Adventure was free, too many kids were riding again and again, so this ticket restricted those under eighteen to one ride per visit.

ADVENTURE THRU INNER SPAC
AND
" MIRACLES FROM MOLECULES "
PRESENTED BY **Monsanto** ADMISSION FREE

continuously, taking "advantage" of the two-passenger, largely enclosed Omnimover vehicles. To discourage couples from doing just whatever it was they were doing in there, Disneyland began including a ticket in each of the Park's ticket books, valid for a single complimentary ride—Guests would have to buy another book of tickets if they wanted to ride the attraction again. When this strategy didn't seem to work, Disneyland increased the speed of the attraction, hoping to shorten the ride time—and the opportunity for amorous mischief. This only led to the attraction's stentorian narration sounding helium-affected in certain zones where the sound track had to speed up to keep pace with the ride vehicles.

Adventure Thru Inner Space went from a free attraction to a "C" ticket in 1972. In 1977, Monsanto's sponsorship expired, and their wondrous display of better living through chemicals that had been the attraction finale was replaced by the Star Traders shop.

Like hippie boots and macramé, over the next eight years, Adventure Thru Inner Space did not age well. Although it had been state-of-the-art on its 1967 opening, the special effects technology had quickly dimmed the attraction's unique qualities, and waiting lines for the attraction became nonexistent.

In the autumn of 1985, after eighteen years of "piercing the wall of the oxygen atom," Adventure Thru Inner Space closed its doors to become the home of Star Tours. To ensure that the optimistic futuristic enthusiasm that was Adventure Thru Inner Space would not be entirely forgotten, Imagineers paid homage to the attraction within Star Tours. In the Droidnostics Center,

one of the R2 units works on a console that was originally one of the dioramas in the queue area of Adventure Thru Inner Space. Also in the Droidnostics Center, one of the original "miniaturized" Atomobiles from the queue dioramas can be seen in a basket on the overhead chain conveyor. Inside the Starspeeder, as guests embark on their journey to the Moon of Endor, they can see the "mighty microscope" lying among some rubble in the scene where Rex crashes through the maintenance hangar.

Walt Disney once said: "A picture is a thing that once you wrap it up and turn it over to Technicolor, you're through. The last picture I just finished, the one I just wrapped up a few weeks ago? It's gone. I can't touch it. There's things in it I don't like. I can't do anything about it. I wanted something live. Something that could grow. Something I could keep 'plussing' with ideas. The Park is that. Not only can I add things, but even the *trees* will keep growing. The thing will get more beautiful every year! And as I find out what the public likes or they don't like, I have to apply that to some other thing. I can't change that picture. So that's why I wanted that park."

Adventure Thru Inner Space may be gone, but it is certainly not forgotten.

Go to
Insider
www.Disney.com/DisneyInsider

The Disney That Never Was

DISNEYLAND CONSTRUCTION

LIBERTY STREET
GRAND OPENING 1959

by Jeff Kurtti

"Actually, if you could see close in my eyes, the American flag is waving in both of them and up my spine is growing this red, white and blue stripe."
—*Walt Disney*

Like most Americans of his era, Walt Disney was a shameless patriot. Before the Cold War, political assassinations, Watergate, Monica Lewinsky, and Enron, Americans were far more inclined to believe their leaders, trust their judgment, and together celebrate the ideals and aspirations of the American Dream. Within Disneyland, Walt Disney's idealization of the American spirit is omnipresent, yet one of his longest-planned and most ambitious venerations to the Republic was never built: Disneyland's Liberty Street.

Originally scheduled to open in the autumn of 1957, Liberty Street was founded on Walt Disney's belief that Americans often failed to comprehend the tremendous significance of their heritage. In Liberty Street, Walt intended to dramatize the events of the Revolutionary War period in an entertaining way and provide Disneyland guests with a better understanding of, and sense of pride in, the American way of life.

Liberty Street was designed as a cul-de-sac, extending northeast from Town Square on Main Street, U.S.A. Unlike any other area of the Park at that time, Liberty Street's buildings, exhibits, and presentations were all integral to the total show.

The street was to be an architectural composite of several American cities as they existed in the late 1700s. Cobblestones would pave the way down Liberty Street and into Liberty Square, past shops and exhibits—a blacksmith shop, apothecary, glassmaker, weaver, print shop, insurance office, silversmith, and cabinetmaker—representing the types of enterprises found in America during the Colonial era.

Also to be located in Liberty Street was a scale model of the United States Capitol Building. Once displayed in the Main Street Opera House at Disneyland, Walt Disney had purchased the model from an artisan who had devoted twenty-five years to carving the meticulous replica from stone. Liberty Hall was the centerpiece of the square, and the entrance to the cornerstone attraction, known as One Nation Under God, and comprising the Hall of the Declaration of Independence and the Hall of the Presidents of the United States. A large foyer with dioramas depicting famous scenes of the establishment of American independence would serve as the entry to the twin auditoriums.

The Hall of the Declaration of Independence was to present the stirring and dramatic story of the United States in three scenes, based on three famous American paintings. The Colonial auditorium was designed to seat 500 people on pew-like benches. On the ceiling, thirteen stars representing the thirteen original colonies would light the auditorium. The proscenium would contain three framed settings for the patriotic tableaux, featuring life-size sculpted figures in elaborate costumes and settings.

The first scene, based upon *The Drafting of the Declaration of Independence* by J.L.G. Ferris, would depict Benjamin Franklin and John Adams in consultation with Thomas Jefferson as he drafted the document. As the curtain fell, another would open to reveal *The Signing of the Declaration of Independence*, painted by John Trumbull. The final scene represented Henry Mosler's *Ringing of the Liberty Bell*. Narration, interspersed with quotes from the Declaration, accompanied by a stirring musical score, would tell the story and explain the significance of each tableau.

In the Hall of the Presidents of the United States, stage lights would gradually brighten and curtains partially open to reveal in silhouette the life-size sculptured and costumed figures of George Washington and the presidents immediately succeeding him. Martial music would begin as theatrical lighting played across the famous visage of Washington, creating a feeling of reality. Narration of the trials, decisions, and formation of America's heritage was to be complemented by excerpts from presidential speeches. At the stirring conclusion, all of the nation's thirty-four presidents would be seen on the enormous stage, behind them a rear-projected dimensional image of the United States Capitol Building, as clouds drifted across the twilight sky, and a grand musical finale brought the show to a close.

The concept of Liberty Street and its attractions depended heavily on the credibility of its human portrayals and the development of a nascent figure-animation technology

OPPOSITE: A sign of things not to come. Despite this bold banner, Liberty Street never had a grand opening in 1959 or any other year.

ABOVE: Evocative conceptual art envisioned the Colonial era style and atmosphere of the proposed Liberty Street.

141

LEFT: Many tests and much Imagineering effort had Mr. Lincoln ready to make a dramatic debut at the 1964–1965 New York World's Fair after less than two years' intensive work.

ABOVE: Dramatic conceptual art by Sam McKim helped set the stage for Great Moments with Mr. Lincoln.

BELOW: A striking mural of a great quote from Mr. Lincoln welcomed visitors to the Illinois Pavilion at the New York World's Fair.

known as Audio-Animatronics, whereby music, voices, and sound effects could be synchronized to the actions of three-dimensional figures and objects. New technology in stereophonic sound, automated show lighting, narration, and presentation staging would enhance the feeling of reality in both auditorium presentations. But in 1957, the technology necessary to present the One Nation Under God show did not exist, and rather than risk indignity and ridicule, the entire concept was shelved.

WED Enterprises (now known as Walt Disney Imagineering) began to produce prototype technology, including the head of Confucius for a proposed Chinese restaurant in Adventureland, the entire feathered cast of Walt Disney's Enchanted Tiki Room, and the first figure for the Hall of the Presidents of the United States—Abraham Lincoln.

When the promoter and president of the 1964–1965 New York World's Fair, Robert Moses came to the Walt Disney Studio for an update on Disney's work on the Ford and General Electric pavilions for the Fair, he saw the Lincoln figure and, awestruck, demanded a demonstration.

Walt explained that the technology was embryonic, and years away from the perfection required to perform dozens of times a day. Nevertheless, after watching the Lincoln figure "come to life," Moses insisted that it would premiere at the World's Fair.

Although Lincoln's technological bugs delayed its New York debut by a week, Great Moments with Mr. Lincoln at the State of Illinois pavilion was a tremendous hit. The public had never seen anything like it, and the quality of showmanship demanded by Walt Disney had many audience members convinced that Disney's "robotic" Lincoln was actually an actor. A second figure was created for permanent display in Disneyland. It opened in 1965 in the Main Street Opera House, just a few feet away from the original planned location of Liberty Street. Lincoln held forth in this venue for nearly four decades.

Shortly after the closing of the 1964–1965 New York World's Fair, WED began work on Magic Kingdom Park at Walt Disney World in Florida. One major difference from its California counterpart was that the Florida park incorporated a variation on the original 1957 Liberty Street, redesigned and renamed Liberty Square.

Located off the hub at the northwest compass point of the Magic Kingdom, Liberty Square boasts three major attractions: the *Liberty Belle* Riverboat, The Haunted Mansion, and the single survivor of the original Disneyland Liberty Street concept, The Hall of Presidents.

Although as recently as 1990 Disneyland announced plans for Liberty Street, current plans do not include such an addition. Guests do experience the pages of American history through The Hall of Presidents at Magic Kingdom Park and The American Adventure in World Showcase at Epcot. Each attraction both educates and entertains as only Disney can—with liberty and justice for all.

LEFT: Mr. Lincoln again took center stage when the Hall of Presidents debuted in Liberty Square in Magic Kingdom Park at Walt Disney World in 1971—bringing things full circle to the original presidential attraction planned for Disneyland Park's never-realized Liberty Street.

Animation Rarities

An Inside Look

by Leonard Maltin

There are so many facets to Walt's Disney's life and career that I don't think fans or aficionados will ever run out of material.

The same might be said for his film vault. Just when you think you've seen it all, there are more nuggets to be mined. That's why I'm so pleased that I was able to compile the *Rarities* collection for our Walt Disney Treasures DVD series.

This package also provided me with an opportunity to include some examples of Walt's first successful series, the *Alice* comedies. I've always been impressed with these silent shorts; I've seen them with modern audiences and people really respond to them. Several years ago, I hosted a showing of the 1924 version of *Peter Pan* at the El Capitan theater in Hollywood, and the extra added attraction was *Alice's Wild West Show*. It went over like gangbusters, and when the original Alice, Virginia Davis, appeared on stage afterward, the crowd went wild. (I think viewers who've never encountered Virginia will feel the same way after watching our conversations on the DVD.)

The ingredients that always stood Disney in good stead—a simple story premise and lots of gags—are already in evidence in these one-reelers. Walt and his Kansas City colleagues were steeped in the tradition of silent-film comedy, and also absorbed the lessons to be learned from their more established rivals in the world of animated cartoons, such as Max Fleischer and Paul Terry. What's more, while the interaction between the live little girl and her cartoon friends is elemental, it's still fun to watch—and surprisingly successful, even in this age of computer-generated special effects.

The coming of sound marked the first great turning point in Walt Disney's career, and early "talkie" shorts such as "Steamboat Willie" and "The Skeleton Dance" cemented the Studio's reputation as a leader in the cartoon field. Earlier releases in the Walt Disney Treasures series enable you to trace the progress of animation in both the Mickey Mouse and "Silly Symphonies" series of the 1930s.

As Walt geared up for feature-film production, short subjects were relegated to an also-ran position for the first time. Nothing ever left the Studio without Walt's involvement and personal seal of approval, but after *Snow White and the Seven Dwarfs* the shorts no longer commanded his full attention.

Still, there were exceptions along the way. The great popularity of Munro Leaf's *Ferdinand the Bull*, published in 1936 (and illustrated by Robert Lawson) inspired Walt to acquire rights to the storybook and adapt it for the screen. Released as a one-shot item, not an entry in the "Silly Symphonies," this charming tale of a bull who refuses to fight became a great hit, won an Academy Award, and gave Disney a character that people remembered for years to come, even though he never made another screen appearance. (There were even Ferdinand the Bull books, records, drinking glasses, toys, games, figurines, puppets, pins, coloring books, and greeting cards.)

Animation buffs have always had a special fondness for this short because of its "in" jokes: the picadors are broad caricatures of various Disney animators, while the matador is generally believed to be a rendering of Walt himself.

144

LEFT: Walt's silent "Alice Comedies" were his first big success.

BELOW: The "Silly Symphonies" brought color and music to motion picture audiences enraptured with the rapidly growing art of animation.

During World War II, when the Studio was humming with activity as a production center for training, instructional, and morale-building films, other ideas would hatch that seemed to demand a niche of their own. That's why Walt commissioned production of "Chicken Little" and "The Pelican and the Snipe." Each one had a particular point to make to wartime audiences on the home front.

"Chicken Little"—which bears scant relationship to the 2005 Disney feature of the same name—is sometimes mistakenly thought to be a straight rendering of the famous fable. In fact, it's a wartime parable about the risk of readily believing unfounded rumors, and its finale is unusually grim for a cartoon—though entirely appropriate to get its point across. Remember, our country was at war, and there was palpable concern at that time about enemy sabotage.

"The Pelican and the Snipe" doesn't try to sell a message, but it does take place during wartime, when the seemingly innocuous "sleepwalking" of a pelican becomes risky business, causing his pal the snipe no end of trouble. The story takes place off the coast of Uruguay, another indicator of its time period, as the United States was making the most of its Good Neighbor Policy and focusing attention on Central and South America. (That's what inspired the Disney films *Saludos Amigos* and *The Three Caballeros*.)

In some cases, the inspiration for a short came from an outside source, like Virginia Lee Burton's enduringly popular children's book *The Little House* or Ellis Parker Butler's *Pigs Is Pigs*. The Studio had already turned to classic American tall tales such as Pecos Bill a decade before Paul Bunyan came along, so perhaps it was felt that his time had come. One can also picture Disney artists and story men developing character ideas for Donald Duck or Goofy shorts that may have led to the creation of full-fledged shorts "Morris the Midget Moose" and "Lambert, the Sheepish Lion."

The fate of short subjects changed yet again in the early 1950s, as the entire movie industry underwent tremendous upheaval. A United States court decree demanded that movie studios separate themselves from their theater chains—which meant that RKO movies (including Walt's cartoons) could no longer be guaranteed automatic bookings in RKO theaters. Pressure was also brought to bear on the practice of "block booking," forcing independent theater owners to take an entire slate or season of movies (including short subjects and cartoons) in order to get the handful of plums they really wanted.

Television put the last nail in the coffin of the old studio system. Radio had been seen as a competitor when it came along in the 1920s, but that furor had settled down when TV reared its head in the late 1940s. By the early 1950s, people were changing their habits of going to the movies once or twice a week because they had so much free entertainment at home.

Even with these changes, most theater owners knew that

CLOCKWISE, FROM TOP LEFT: Originally planned as a "Silly Symphony," "Ferdinand the Bull" was ultimately released as a "special," to great popularity and an Academy Award as the Best Cartoon of 1938. Disney favorite Sterling Holloway voiced the "me" in "Ben and Me," Amos Mouse. The tall tale of "Paul Bunyan" was the perfect subject for Disney animation. "The Little House" featured the stylish designs of Mary Blair. Six decades before Disney's computer-animated feature, Walt Disney produced "Chicken Little" as a cartoon short that was actually a wartime exploration of mass hysteria and paranoia.

audiences were in the habit of seeing newsreels and cartoons with their feature films; they just didn't want to pay any more to book them than they had ten years earlier.

Walt Disney had always spent more than he stood to make back on his cartoons because he insisted on the highest quality of production. Now he was forced to take another look at the reality of the situation, and in the 1950s he phased out his long-running Mickey Mouse, Goofy, and Donald Duck series.

But it didn't make sense to wipe short subjects off the slate entirely. For one thing, Walt had animators, inkers, painters, and other artists on staff fifty-two weeks a year. He couldn't have them sitting idle when work slowed down or stopped on a feature film. What's more, once he decided to open his own distribution company, Buena Vista, he felt that Disney features should be accompanied by Disney shorts and featurettes, rather than leaving the accompaniment to a theater owner's whim.

That's why just when the rest of Hollywood was phasing out short-subject production; Walt Disney entered a new period of producing these mini-movies. If a story demanded more than six or seven minutes' time (like a Goofy cartoon) that wasn't an issue: "Pigs Is Pigs" ran ten minutes, "Ben and Me," twenty.

It must have been especially satisfying for Walt to see so many of these pint-sized productions earn Academy Award nominations. (For the record, those nominees were "Lambert, the Sheepish Lion," "Pigs Is Pigs," "The Truth About Mother Goose," "Noah's Ark," "Goliath II," and "A Symposium on Popular Songs." Only "Toot, Whistle, Plunk and Boom" actually won the coveted prize.)

Just as the 1930s shorts served as a research-and-design laboratory for new visual ideas and techniques, those one-shot cartoons of the 1950s enabled Walt's artists and story men to stretch their wings and try out bold new ideas.

"Melody" and "Toot, Whistle, Plunk and Boom" allowed directors Ward Kimball and Charles Nichols, along with famed graphic stylist Eyvind Earle, to experiment with a modern design that wouldn't have readily suited a Donald Duck cartoon. Earle's bold, imaginative graphics still look striking and fresh today.

These two cartoons also served as a proving ground for such new formats as the wide-screen CinemaScope process (which required Disney artists to fill the oblong frame in interesting and even humorous ways), 3-D (which demanded visual ideas that would literally pop off the screen), and stereophonic sound. In the latter case, it wasn't so much a matter of Disney keeping up with technology as the other way around. Remember, the initial release of *Fantasia* in 1940 was presented in Fantasound, a pioneering use of stereo surround sound. Some theater owners balked at bearing the cost of installing new equipment for the film, but by the early 1950s fierce competition from TV forced exhibitors to rethink that kind of investment. Listen to the sound track of "Toot" and try to imagine how exciting it must have been to hear various instruments coming from different sides of the theater.

Later in the decade, longtime studio hands Bill Justice (best remembered for his work with Chip and Dale) and X. Atencio started fooling around with stop-motion animation. Walt encouraged them, which led to several charming shorts such as "Jack and Old Mac" and "Noah's Ark."

The Sherman Brothers were delighted to have an opportunity to write Tin Pan Alley tunes simulating the pop styles of every decade of the twentieth century for "A Symposium on Popular Songs." (Richard Sherman discusses this enjoyable—and memorable—assignment on the commentary track of the new DVD.) Bill Justice and X. Atencio illustrated these evocative songs with the most delightfully designed animated paper cutouts, while Paul Frees went to town performing some of these ditties in the guise of Professor Ludwig Von Drake.

Simply reading the credits on these shorts, spanning several decades, reaffirms the continuity that set the Walt Disney Studio apart from all others. You'll see many of the same names—including those of Walt's famous animators, the "Nine Old Men"—that brought glory to the Disney feature-length films.

Two of the most endearing, if unsung, contributors to the Disney legacy also make a major contribution to the shorts in this collection: voice artists Sterling Holloway and Bill Thompson.

Of the two, Holloway is the more familiar, as his voice was so distinctive and his credits so prominent. Disney fans know him from jobs as diverse as the voice of Mr. Stork in *Dumbo* (1941), the crafty Kaa in *The Jungle Book* (1967), and the beloved Winnie the Pooh. He also lends his talents to a number of shorts, including "The Pelican and the Snipe," "Lambert, the Sheepish Lion," and "Ben and Me."

Thompson is less celebrated, in part because he did much of his work anonymously, and in part

because he used a variety of voices in his work. Radio fans knew him as the voice of Wallace Whimple on the long-running series *Fibber McGee and Molly*; cartoon fans of several generations would immediately know him as the voice of MGM's cartoon star Droopy. Disney fans would probably cite The White Rabbit in *Alice in Wonderland*, Mr. Smee in *Peter Pan*, and Jock in *Lady and the Tramp* as his most illustrious assignments, but after watching this selection of shorts you may also think of him as Professor Owl in "Melody" and "Toot, Whistle, Plunk and Boom" and Ranger Audubon J. Woodlore in the Humphrey Bear cartoons of the 1950s.

Spanning some forty years, these films still provide a great deal of entertainment as well as a cavalcade of changing styles and techniques in the world of animation. Although some of them may not rank among his most famous or ambitious work, they are more than a mere footnote to Walt Disney's career.

TOP: An accomplished musician and founder of the famed Dixieland jazz troupe, legendary animator Ward Kimball co-directed the artistically experimental shorts "Adventures in Music: Melody" and the Oscar-winning "Toot, Whistle, Plunk and Boom" (right and left, below).

MIDDLE: The voice of Professor Owl in Adventures in "Music: Melody" and "Toot, Whistle, Plunk and Boom," Bill Thompson provided voices for many other Disney productions. Here, the versatile voice artist vocalizes the role of the Dodo in *Alice in Wonderland*.

148

Walt Disney Treasures
Disney Rarities
Celebrated Shorts 1920s-1960s

Disney Rarities: Celebrated Shorts 1920s–1960s showcases a collection of Walt Disney's outstanding animated shorts—many of which are unknown by even Disney aficionados, and are seeing their first-ever DVD release. Included are several of Walt's "Alice Comedies," a pioneering series of early short films that combined live action and animation. These wonderful, lesser-known unique films pre-date much of the work that would make him world-famous.

Bonus features include: Alice's Cartoon World, in which Leonard Maltin discusses Disney's historic "Alice" shorts with Virginia Davis (who played the original Alice when she was four years old); From Kansas City to Hollywood, a timeline of Walt's silent era; "A Feather in His Collar," a rarely seen short supporting the Community Chest; audio commentary for "A Symposium on Popular Songs" by composer Richard Sherman; and still-frame galleries.

Go to
Insider
www.Disney.com/DisneyInsider

ASK DAVE

Dave Smith, director of the Walt Disney Archives, brings more than thirty-five years of Disney experience to answering questions about Disney history, art, music, characters, people, places, and things from Disney Insiders around the world.

Where did Disney find the house used in **Pollyanna**?

In order to find a home most closely resembling architecture in the eastern United States during the early 1900s, Walt Disney's location scouts found an ideal house to serve as the dwelling of Aunt Polly Harrington. It was in Santa Rosa, in the Napa Valley of northern California. The house, known as the Mableton Mansion, occupied a full block in the center of town and was surrounded by spacious lawns and gardens. It is a replica of a Natchez, Mississippi, antebellum house originally built in 1877, and that still stands today.

When watching **The One and Only, Genuine, Original Family Band** *recently, did I recognize the boy that played young Jason Walton on TV in* **The Waltons?**

Yes, indeed you did. That was Jon Walmsley, who also provided the voice of Christopher Robin in *Winnie the Pooh and the Blustery Day.*

Was there really a segment produced for the original **Fantasia** *that was never used?*

The Disney animators created a segment to illustrate Debussy's "Clair de Lune," but Walt Disney eventually decided that the piece did not fit, so the animation was shelved. But when *Make Mine Music* was in production a few years later, the animation was brought out again but used with the song "Blue Bayou" instead of "Clair de Lune." The original "Clair de Lune" segment was discovered and restored by film preservationist Scott MacQueen and made available as bonus material on *The Fantasia Legacy* DVD.

Didn't Fess Parker, Disney's Davy Crockett, also have a long-running Daniel Boone series?

Most people do not realize that despite the worldwide popularity of the initial Davy Crockett shows, there were only five of them. It was one of the world's first miniseries, initially with three shows telling the story of Davy's life from his Indian-fighting days to his death at the Alamo. But, by the time the third episode had aired, the character had become so popular that Walt Disney resurrected him the following season for two shows based on the legends of Davy. Fess Parker did indeed star in a six season *Daniel Boone* television series from 1964–1970. It was not for Disney, but rather a 20th Century Fox series for NBC. However, Disney did have its own *Daniel Boone* television four-parter in 1960–1961, starring Dewey Martin as the frontiersman.

I know The Mickey Mouse Club's Annette made many films while she was under contract to Disney. Where did he discover her?

When Annette Funicello was twelve years old, she appeared on an amateur program at the Starlight Bowl in Burbank, California. Walt Disney happened to catch the performance, entitled "Ballet vs. Jive," and this led to her selection as one of the original Mouseketeers. Her first public appearance as a Mouseketeer was at the opening of Disneyland on July 17, 1955.

Since Jodie Foster, who recently starred in Flightplan, was a child actor for Disney, does she have the Disney record for the most number of years between her first and most recent acting roles for the Studio?

Foster starred first for Disney in *Menace on the Mountain* in 1970, giving her thirty-five years. But she is beat by Kurt Russell with thirty-nine years (between *Follow Me, Boys!* in 1966 and *Sky High* in 2005), and Glynis Johns with forty-two years. Johns, perhaps best remembered as Mrs. Banks in *Mary Poppins*, starred in *The Sword and the Rose* in 1953, with her most recent Disney work the Touchstone release *While You Were Sleeping* in 1995.

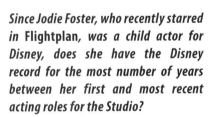

Was that really movie actor Ronald Colman's voice in the Donald Duck cartoon "Donald's Double Trouble"?

In that cartoon, where Donald tries to impress Daisy with a double with impeccable manners and a perfect voice, actor Leslie Denison was hired to imitate Ronald Colman, whose movie roles tended to be well-bred Englishmen. Many times Disney cartoons included caricatures of stars, but imitators always provided their voices. In fact, in "The Autograph Hound," actor/singer Peter Lind Hayes (*The 5,000 Fingers of Dr. T*) did the voices of Robert Taylor, Charlie McCarthy, Groucho Marx, Edward G. Robinson, Joe E. Brown, Ronald Colman, Gary Cooper, Lionel Barrymore, Bing Crosby, Bob Burns, Hugh Herbert, Charles Laughton, and Clark Gable.

Can you give me some background on Walt Disney's family?

Walt Disney's ancestors originated from the town of Isigny-sur-Mer in France. Their name of "d'Isigny" was anglicized to "Disney" after they traveled to England with William the Conqueror. Centuries later, the family moved to Ireland. Walt's great-grandfather crossed the Atlantic from Ireland to Canada in 1834, where he settled in Ontario and built a gristmill. Walt's father, Elias, was born in Canada, but while in his teens moved with his family to Kansas. A few years later when a neighbor family named Call moved to Florida, Elias went with them and soon married their daughter, Flora. Elias and Flora had bad luck growing oranges and running a hotel, so they moved to Chicago where Elias became a building contractor. It was there that Walt was born, on December 5, 1901. Most people do not realize that Walt's father was Canadian; Elias did not become a naturalized American citizen until late in his life.

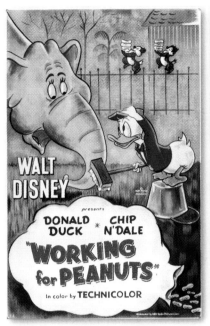

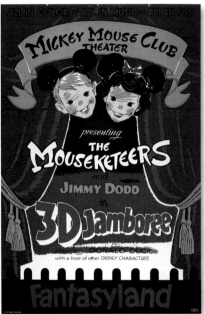

Mickey's PhilharMagic *at Magic Kingdom Park at Walt Disney World is great; when did Walt Disney first experiment with 3-D?*

Back in the 1950s, when 3-D was first introduced, Walt Disney made the first-ever 3-D cartoon, *Adventures in Music: Melody* (1953). It was followed by a Donald Duck cartoon, *Working for Peanuts* (1953), and a program shown at Disneyland called *3D Jamboree* (1956). Disney did not produce any more 3-D films until *Magic Journeys* was created for Journey into Imagination at Epcot in 1982. This was followed by *Captain EO* in 1986, *Muppet*Vision 3D* in 1991, *Honey, I Shrunk the Audience* in 1997 (known in Japan as *Micro-Adventure*), and *It's Tough to Be a Bug!* in 1999. The recent feature *Chicken Little* was adapted to 3-D for release in selected theaters.

***Spin and Marty** on **The Mickey Mouse Club** has always been one of my favorites. How many episodes were made in all?*

There were three different Spin and Marty serials. The first, *The Adventures of Spin and Marty*, had twenty-five episodes; the second, *The Further Adventures of Spin and Marty*, had twenty-three; and the third, *The New Adventures of Spin and Marty*, had thirty. Thus, there were seventy-eight total episodes.

When did Disney start its Buena Vista Distribution Company?

The Living Desert (1953) was the initial film distributed by Buena Vista, created when Disney's previous distributor, RKO, showed no confidence in the film's success. *The Living Desert*, Disney's first feature-length True-Life Adventure, of course, went on to win an Oscar and proved a fitting beginning for the new company.

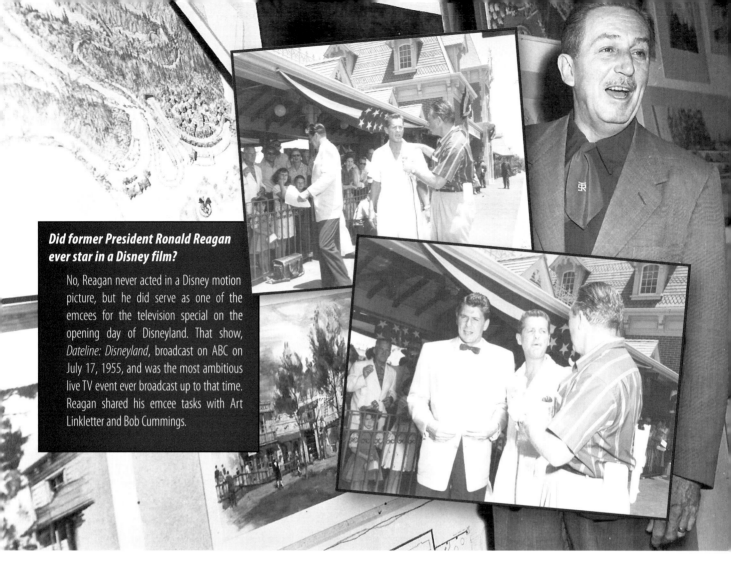

Did former President Ronald Reagan ever star in a Disney film?

No, Reagan never acted in a Disney motion picture, but he did serve as one of the emcees for the television special on the opening day of Disneyland. That show, *Dateline: Disneyland*, broadcast on ABC on July 17, 1955, and was the most ambitious live TV event ever broadcast up to that time. Reagan shared his emcee tasks with Art Linkletter and Bob Cummings.

If Goofy and Pluto are both dogs, why are they so different?

The Disney artists created Pluto as a pet dog, and he possesses all the characteristics of a dog. Goofy, on the other hand, was created as a human character that just happens to have some of the features of a dog.

I remember hearing a September date for Mickey Mouse's debut, but now you use November 18. Why?

Back in the 1930s special promotions were held in theaters for Mickey's birthday, and convenient Saturday dates were arbitrarily chosen so the theaters could attract large audiences of children. But the "birth" of Mickey Mouse was always said to be when "Steamboat Willie," his first film seen by the public, premiered at the Colony Theater in New York. One of my early tasks after establishing the Archives in 1970 was to research that date, and I discovered that it was actually November 18, 1928. So ever since then, that date has been promoted as Mickey's debut.

Did Walt Disney attend an art school, or was he self-taught?

Walt Disney attended some evening art classes in Kansas City and Chicago while he was growing up, and he served on the art staff for his high school's magazine, *The Voice*. He was talented as an artist and seemed to have a knack for adding humor to his drawings. After starting his company in Hollywood, however, he came to realize that others could animate better than he, so he turned instead to story work and direction.

I think the Disney "Silly Symphony" cartoons are masterpieces; how many of them were made?

There were a total of seventy-five "Silly Symphonies," from "The Skeleton Dance" in 1929 to "The Ugly Duckling" in 1939. Based on musical themes, classic stories, and unique characters, this series was used by Walt Disney to give his animators practice so they could eventually turn their skills to making animated feature films.

What does the improper fraction 10/6 on the Mad Hatter's hat mean?

That is not a fraction, but the price tag, which the scatterbrained Mad Hatter evidently forgot to remove from his hat, and its use is based on original Tenniel illustrations for Lewis Carroll's 1865 book, *Alice's Adventures in Wonderland*. 10/6 is the way the English used to write ten shillings, six pence. Of course, now that the English have switched to a decimal system, they don't use shillings anymore.

Does the drop at Splash Mountain in Disneyland really go straight down from five stories?

The drop is at a forty-seven-degree angle. The fifty-two-and-one-half-foot drop (equivalent to a five-story building) was, at Splash Mountain's opening, the longest water-flume chute in the world.

Joe Grant

Joe Grant started with Disney in October of 1937 doing character design on Snow White and the Seven Dwarfs. *He was a m[...] the long-defunct Character Model Department; it was said that no model sheet was official until it bore the seal "O.K., J.G."*

Joe was an artist, writer, designer, and, at one time, a producer—the Studio's authority on the design and appearance [...] everything that moved on the screen. He worked on such classics as Snow White and the Seven Dwarfs, Pinocchio, Fanta[...] Reluctant Dragon *(Baby Weems sequence),* Dumbo, Saludos Amigos, Make Mine Music, *and* Alice in Wonderland.

In 1949, Joe took a forty-year "leave of absence" from the Studio when the Character Model Department disbanded to [...] economic concerns brought on by World War II, and started up the successful ceramics studio Opechee Designs and the greeting c[...] pany, Castle Ltd. In 1989, he returned to Disney to work on Beauty and the Beast, *for which he contributed gags for the househo[...] and other characters in the film. He continued to work full-time for Disney for the next sixteen years and contributed to* Alad[...] Lion King, Pocahontas, The Hunchback of Notre Dame, Hercules, *and* Mulan. *Grant also came up with the yo-yo playing flar[...]* Fantasia/2000 *and the title for Disney/Pixar's film* Monsters, Inc. *Joe passed away on May 6, 2005, at the age of ninety-six.*

by Mike Gabriel

Falling in love with a guy already in his eighties was a dangerous thing. It's like guaranteeing you are going to get hurt when they "go." We all knew Joe was old, but he never acted, looked, thought, or drew like he was old, so we convinced ourselves that he wasn't old at all. He would live forever.

But how many times, when I was alone pondering the deep truths of life, like when I was jogging in the morning, did I think "Uh-oh! Joe is old. Joe is really old. And now, after years of showing no sign of acting old, he is finally starting to slow down and get a bit weak of limb. Not Joe! The rock! The Fountain of Youth! And I am so wrapped up in loving Joe more than anyone outside my family, that, boy, when he dies I am going to be in big-hurt land. I am in serious emotional jeopardy. I am in big trouble. Someday he will die—most likely before me—and I will be really hurting."

Well, I would always—and I mean always—say to myself, "Hell, he will probably live longer than I will. For all I know, I will get some deadly form of cancer and die in two weeks, and Joe will live to be 106 years old, so don't sweat it, dude. Relax. Joe ain't going anywhere for a long time. He ain't even 100 yet. He has a long way to go."

The news hit hard on Friday afternoon. Joe is dead. We just had lunch the day before at our usual place, Genio's in Burbank, with the kindest, most loving, giving friend Joe could have, Burny Mattinson. The three of us had more laughs than usual that day. Joe was in an especially good mood, and seemed fit and definitely as sound as ever in mind and wit. He could make me laugh more than anyone I have ever met. His wit and whimsy were infectious and intoxicating and addictive. But he was all Joe that day, and we all had absolutely no clue that Joe was about to leave us.

Joe Grant was as timeless as his ideas. He never dated himself. He stayed contemporary. He stayed in the pr[...] He didn't bury himself in past victories; he strove to c[...] with new and better victories. He liked being with tale[...] people who shared his love of great animated films. An[...] he could add to help others make great films, he woul[...] He gave all he had to give with every bit of strength h[...] within his slender, strong frame. He forced every bit o[...] and sinew to never give up. Even though his brain wou[...] tell him it was hopeless, his heart and creative spirit forced him to continue. He loved being with us all. He[...] loved helping us all make better films than we could without him. He was selfless and didn't have an ego. He was focused on the film and what would improve it—nothing more.

Joe was the only guy who lived as an active part of both golden ages of Disney animation. The *only* active participant. The only guy. Joe lived through an entire generation of friends growing old and dying. But that didn't stop Joe from looking forward

and making new friends from the next generation. Good, deep, honest friends, who loved him, and he loved them. That is Joe. Bury the past and get on with the future. Keep going into the next thing. How many times did Joe say how marvelous some new animated show or movie or computer tool was? There is endless curiosity and wonder if you keep looking ahead. Boy, if that doesn't feel like a Walt Disney way of looking at this world. When you were with Joe, you could always feel the same sensibility in him that was in the Disney classics we grew up loving. That was simply because this was the guy who put so much of himself into those films. He was the guy. He was every bit a main ingredient to the Disney magic.

Joe Grant wasn't a legend to me. He wasn't the great Joe Grant; he was my friend Joe Grant. The guy I wanted to see every day and go to lunch with and just shoot the day's news with Joe Grant. He was a guy I loved being with. He was the best in every conceivable way. I can't imagine my life without Joe in it. In the fifteen some years I have known him, he has redefined my ideas about art and what makes art professional and not amateurish. He would never push a drawing to its extreme. He would let it be solid and strong and supremely clear in its subtle-yet-definite attack. It was solid and not desperate to impress or exaggerated to the point of insult. His work would let the viewer see the story point within without beating them over the head with it. It was respectful. Mature. Tasteful. Sophisticated. And above all else, it was insightful—which made it so entertaining.

Joe taught us all how to live, and now he has taught us all how to die. With grace, dignity and class. Ninety-six years was not near enough Joe for me. I wanted more. He gave all he had to give to us, and to this Studio. That is all he had to give. Who could ask for more? Me. It wasn't enough for me, but it was all we are going to get of Joe.

Thank you, Joe, for coming back home to Disney and letting us all be a part of you and your brilliance. You have taught us all a thousand things without ever once trying to teach us anything. You merely wanted to be with us and be one of us. But that was impossible. You never would just be one of us, Joe. You were too special and too brilliant. You were our link to Walt and the best that Disney ever was then and now. Thank you for coming back. You broke our hearts, but it was worth it. And because of you, there will be a slew of ninety-five-year-old artists in the future, toiling away in the animation industry, trying to attain the unattainable. To be like Joe.

THIS PAGE: A sampling of the prolific Joe Grant's unique approach to greeting cards and ceramics.

Joe Ranft

Joe Ranft, one of the key creators of Pixar's hit animated features and the voice of Heimlich the Bavarian caterpillar in A Bug's L
1998), died in an automobile accident on August 16, 2005. He was forty-five.

Ranft was widely respected as one of the top story artists in the animation industry. He was one of seven writers nominated for
Academy Award for best original screenplay for 1995's Toy Story, but Ranft spent most of his time drawing storyboards for anima
films. Telling stories in one form or another was Ranft's lifelong passion. Born in Pasadena, he grew up in Whittier, where his early intere
included movies, drawing, performing in school plays, and doing sleight-of-hand magic.

Ranft entered the character animation program at California Institute of the Arts in the fall of 1978. As a student, he was inspi
by Bill Peet's storyboards from the 1946 Disney feature Song of the South.

Ranft left CalArts for the Walt Disney Studio in 1980, where he quickly established a reputation as an exceptional story artist. Wh
at Disney, Ranft became friends with John Lasseter, who later became a top executive at Pixar Animation Studios.

Ranft moved to Pixar to serve as story supervisor on Lasseter's Toy Story, the first computer-animated feature. His understand
of story structure and his talent for creating emotionally complex characters that audiences cared about won him a place in the core gro
of artists at Pixar.

by Brenda Chapman

look back over my twenty years of friendship with Joe and I
can't, for the life of me, remember the moment that I met him.
It seems like I've just always known him—and I thank whatever
higher power there might be that I did know him. I would not
be who I am, *what* I am, if it were not for Joe. And I know that
there is an amazing number of people out there who would say
the same.

He came wandering through CalArts one night, in my
third year there, and stopped by to say "Hello." He saw my
storyboards for my film up on the wall. "Hey! Those are
pretty good! Have you thought about going into story?" Oddly
enough, I hadn't. (I was doing that "animator" thing like everyone else was.) That was the decisive moment of my career.

I started working with Joe at Disney back in 1987–1988
(it's all a bit fuzzy right now), sharing an office in the old
Mermaid trailer on Flower Street in Development. He was trying to come up with different ways to put Mickey Mouse into
a featurette. Not something he was very excited about. He
amazed me, even then, how he could dislike doing something
so much and be optimistic about it at the same time. Maybe
it helped that he watched me be stuck on something even
worse—trying to board Mickey and Donald public service
announcements. Just a couple of weeks ago, he leaned over
at lunch and started singing softly "Buckle up, Unca Donald,
buckle up. Quack! Quack!" just to watch my horrified reaction.

Joe always managed to pop up in key moments in my life,
kind of like the guru that shows up in a story. Like when he

was down in L.A. to do a story talk at Disney a couple of yea
ago—at a point in my life where I didn't know what I wanted
to do—the joy of my work was gone. Joe invited me to sit in
He was so passionate, so in love with storytelling—he actual
got choked up while he talked about it. It took my breath awa
that after all these years, he could look past all the bad stuff
and feel the joy of telling a good story and what that would
mean to an audience. And even more, what it could mean to
an individual in the audience. The stories he told and the stori
he loved touched him in some deep way. He wanted to give
that back. And he did.

It was only a few months after that talk at Disney that Jo
called me to see if I'd come up here to work with him on Cars

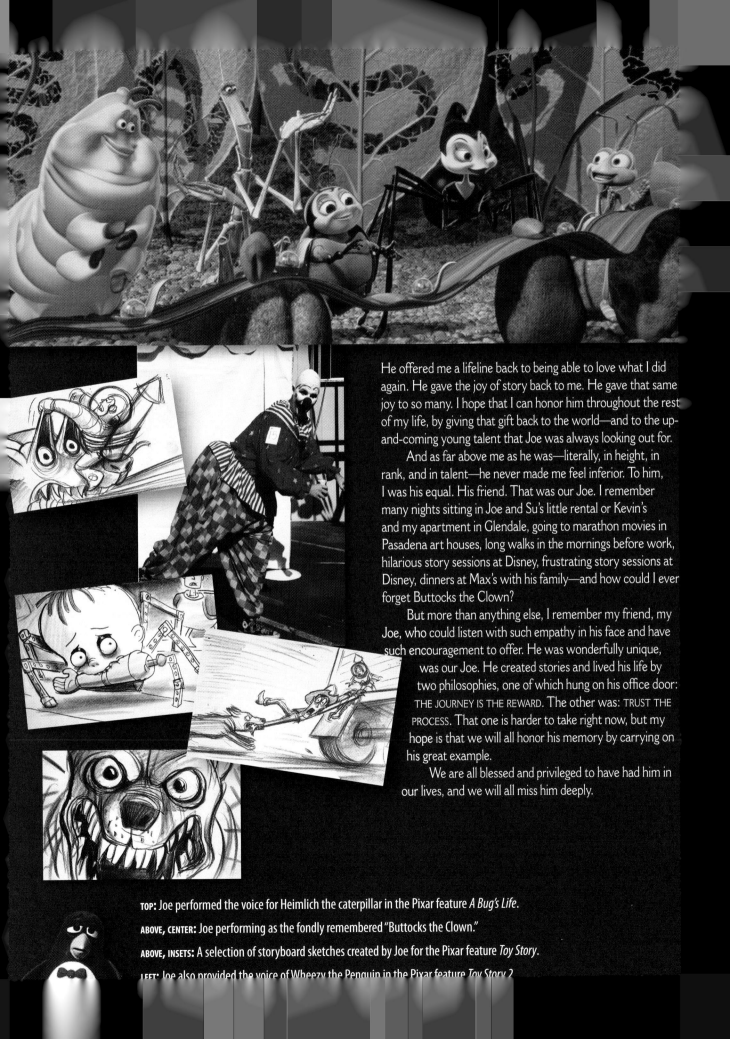

He offered me a lifeline back to being able to love what I did again. He gave the joy of story back to me. He gave that same joy to so many. I hope that I can honor him throughout the rest of my life, by giving that gift back to the world—and to the up-and-coming young talent that Joe was always looking out for.

And as far above me as he was—literally, in height, in rank, and in talent—he never made me feel inferior. To him, I was his equal. His friend. That was our Joe. I remember many nights sitting in Joe and Su's little rental or Kevin's and my apartment in Glendale, going to marathon movies in Pasadena art houses, long walks in the mornings before work, hilarious story sessions at Disney, frustrating story sessions at Disney, dinners at Max's with his family—and how could I ever forget Buttocks the Clown?

But more than anything else, I remember my friend, my Joe, who could listen with such empathy in his face and have such encouragement to offer. He was wonderfully unique, was our Joe. He created stories and lived his life by two philosophies, one of which hung on his office door: THE JOURNEY IS THE REWARD. The other was: TRUST THE PROCESS. That one is harder to take right now, but my hope is that we will all honor his memory by carrying on his great example.

We are all blessed and privileged to have had him in our lives, and we will all miss him deeply.

TOP: Joe performed the voice for Heimlich the caterpillar in the Pixar feature *A Bug's Life*.

ABOVE, CENTER: Joe performing as the fondly remembered "Buttocks the Clown."

ABOVE, INSETS: A selection of storyboard sketches created by Joe for the Pixar feature *Toy Story*.

LEFT: Joe also provided the voice of Wheezy the Penguin in the Pixar feature *Toy Story 2*.

Ever since Walt Disney first squeaked for Mickey Mouse in "Steamboat Willie" (1928), Disney animation has been set to the sound emanating from a choir of unforgettable voices. The year 2005 saw the loss of three of Disney's favorite voice artists, each of whom who has gained immortality though his indelible audio characterizations.

WINCHELL WHILE YOU WORK

Though an accomplished actor and a prolific medical inventor—his most famous and important invention being the artificial heart—Paul Winchell is perhaps best known as a ventriloquist. Inspired by the radio great Edgar Bergen, Paul overcame crippling shyness and a serious stutter to become the premier ventriloquist of the early years of television. Hosting a number of network shows with his dummy pal, Jerry Mahoney, Paul also made many guest appearances on such classic TV series as *The Lucy Show* and *The Dick Van Dyke Show*. His talent for acting and voices combined to make Paul a sought-after voice artist for animated shows and commercials, and that path eventually led him to the microphones of the Disney Studios. Winchell performed as the Chinese cat in *The Aristocats* (1970), Boomer the bird in *The Fox and the Hound* (1981), and most memorably as the "bouncy, trouncy, flouncy, pouncy, fun, fun, fun, fun" voice of the one-of-a-kind critter called Tigger.

Paul first voiced Tigger in the Academy Award–winning *Winnie the Pooh and the Blustery Day* (1968). With this debut of the hyperactive tiger, Paul's vocalization made his one of the most recognized voices in the world. In creating voices, Winchell searched for distinguishing idiosyncrasies. For Tigger, he created a slight lisp, punctuating the enthusiastic tiger's voice with his trademark "T-I-double grrrr-R." At the suggestion of his British-born wife, he improvised Tigger's catchphrase of "TTFN—Ta-ta for now." Winchell kept on trooping as Tigger through *Winnie the Pooh: Seasons of Giving* (1999). "I first met Walt Disney twenty-five or thirty years ago," Winchell recalled in a 1988 interview with the Associated Press. "He said, 'We're both in the same business.' Walt gave me a VIP tour of the Studio. I remember people doing voices. I said, 'Gee, that must be fun.' And here I am."

RIGHT: The wonderful thing about Winchell: the versatile ventriloquist and voice actor Paul Winchell gave voice to the one-and-only Tigger in the original Winnie the Pooh featurettes.

Two members of Disney's delightful Pooh repertory company were among the silenced voices this year—and in a stranger-than-fiction coincidence, Paul Winchell, who voiced Tigger, died on June 24th, 2005—the day before John Fiedler, the voice of Piglet, passed on.

SOME PIG!

Balding and with a high-pitched voice, diminutive John Fiedler realized early on he was not going to be a matinee idol. "I knew I was going to be a character actor from the beginning," he said. "With my voice and my looks, I got the milquetoast, nerd parts." On Broadway Fiedler was acclaimed for performing two very different roles—a poker playing pal and a racist— in two very different stage productions, "The Odd Couple" and "Raisin in the Sun." John recreated his roles in the film versions of the plays, and appeared in many other films and TV shows, most notably in *The Bob Newhart Show* as the too-timid Mr. Peterson.

Fiedler appeared in several Disney live-action productions, including *Rascal* (1969), and voiced characters in *Robin Hood* (1973) *The Fox and the Hound* (1981), and *The Emperor's New Groove* (2000) but he will always be best known and best loved for his audio appearances as the "very small animal" Piglet in the Winnie the Pooh films. Personally selected by Walt Disney to vocally perform Pooh's shy friend, Fiedler played Piglet to timid perfection, his already high pitched voice sped up to give Piglet's tone that extra anxious edge. Like Tigger, Piglet debuted in *Winnie the Pooh and the Blustery Day* and Fiedler went on to play the stammering little pig in other featurettes, TV specials, and films, including *Piglet's Big Movie* (2003) right up through *Pooh's Heffalump Movie* (2005). "There are lot of elements of Piglet that are me," John Fiedler said in explaining how he created the lovable vocal characterization "the shyness and the anxieties and the fears."

His voice may be silenced, but John Fiedler's classic Disney performances will continue to create joy forever.

LEFT: In addition to voicing the endearingly timid Piglet, John Fielder appeared on-screen in several live-action Disney productions, including *Rascal* (1969) and "The Mystery in Dracula's Castle" (pictured here), presented on TV's *The Wonderful World of Disney* in 1973.

THURL-Y GRRRRRR-EAT!

You may never have heard the distinctive name of Thurl Ravenscroft before, but you certainly have heard his even-more-distinctive voice. Most famous for his role as Kellogg's Frosted Flakes spokes-tiger Tony, and for singing "You're a Mean One, Mr. Grinch" in the perennial holiday TV special *Dr. Seuss' The Grinch Who Stole Christmas!* (1966), Ravenscroft also lent his deeper-than-deep bass voice to many Disney productions. A true Disney favorite, Thurl and his singing group, the Mello Men, performed vocals for classic Disney animation as early as *Dumbo* (1941). Their most memorable Disney assignment may have been backing up Peggy Lee as the dog pound inmates in *Lady and the Tramp* (1955). "The most fun we [The Mello Men] ever had was singing barbershop for the dogs," Thurl remembered. "Walt wanted the dogs to sing 'Home Sweet Home' from their prison cell—a kennel. But we had to sound like dogs, not people singing like dogs."

Thurl proved himself a versatile actor in a variety of vocal roles, including one of the mice in *Cinderella* (1950), the Captain in *One Hundred and One Dalmatians* (1961), and the Russian cat in *The Aristocats*. One of Thurl's biggest (no pun intended) Disney roles was as the larger-than-life title character in *Paul Bunyan* (1958). Thurl also made many audio cameos, his inimitable baritone booming out a line or two in such classics as *Mary Poppins* (1964), *Winnie the Pooh and the Blustery Day*, and *Bedknobs and Broomsticks* (1971).

At Disneyland, Ravenscroft made many indelible vocal contributions, including the voice of Fritz the German parrot in the Enchanted Tiki Room and Buff the kibitzing buffalo head in Country Bear Jamboree. And in The Haunted Mansion, one of the broken busts in the graveyard scene features his mustachioed face. "Disneyland wouldn't have been, and wouldn't be, the same without him," said former Disneyland Resort president, Jack Lindquist. "His voice was one of the things that made it all come alive." Thurl Ravenscroft was honored as a Disney Legend in 1995.

ABOVE: Thurl Ravenscroft (seen here recording the voice of the Russian cat for *The Aristocats*) is well known as one of the singing busts in The Haunted Mansion at Disneyland.

LEFT: The 2003 live-action film *The Haunted Mansion* saluted Thurl by featuring his face on one of the film's singing busts.

MODEL CITIZEN

BELOW: "Original Imagineer" Fred Joerger at work on a scale model of Matterhorn Mountain at Disneyland, for its 1978 redesign.

Before entranced Disneyland guests could stroll through Sleeping Beauty Castle or board the *Mark Twain* riverboat, those iconic attractions were first handcrafted in miniature by master model maker Fred Joerger. "I was given artists' drawings of an interior set or a building and interpreted them into models," explained Fred. "It's very easy to make something like The Haunted Mansion look good on paper, but if you don't get it into three dimensions first, you may have a disaster. Well, my job was to create the model to avert disaster, which was fun but a challenge."

Walt Disney handpicked Joerger in 1953 to become, along with Harriet Burns and Wathel Rogers, Walt Disney Imagineering's original "model shop." The first model that Joerger made for Disneyland was of the *Mark Twain* riverboat, followed by elaborate three-dimensional renderings of such Disneyland originals as Main Street, U.S.A.; the Jungle Cruise; and the Matterhorn. Joerger also contributed to Walt's films, creating miniature versions of sets for such Disney classics as *20,000 Leagues Under the Sea* (1954) and *Mary Poppins* (1964).

Fred's skill at creating realistic rockwork out of plaster established his reputation as Imagineering's "resident rock expert," as witnessed by the huge Fred-made stones featured on the Jungle Cruise and Big Thunder Mountain Railroad at both Disneyland and Walt Disney World. When asked how he managed to create such convincing rockwork, the soft-spoken, modest Joerger replied, "You just have to learn to think like a rock." Named a Disney Legend in 2001, Fred Joerger was the very model of a rock-solid Disney artist.

MAGICIAN OF MAKEUP

Though his name rolled by in the credits of hundreds of films, Bob Schiffer was not widely known outside of the film industry—but his accomplishments in over three decades as director of makeup and hairstyling at The Walt Disney Studios made him the master of on-screen glamour and enchantment. "Bob was one of the quiet talents who made Hollywood great," said Michael Eisner. "He worked with the legendary stars who we all know by single names—Astaire, Bogart, Welles, Hepburn, Hayworth, Lancaster, Midler, and Hanks. But among people behind the cameras, Bob was a legend himself."

Bob's long career stretched back to the Golden Age of Hollywood, when he perfected his craft on such classics as *A Night at the Opera* and *The Wizard of Oz*. Schiffer brought his wealth of experience—including long associations with glamorous Rita Hayworth and actor-producer Burt Lancaster—to the Walt Disney Studios in 1968, where his makeup brush became a magic wand. Schiffer relished the challenges that could only be found at the Mouse Factory. From transforming Dean Jones into a hairy hound in *The Shaggy D.A.* and Jeff Bridges into a computer-game pawn in *Tron* to changing Daryl Hannah into a mermaid in *Splash*, Bob took his already illustrious career to a fantastic new level. Honored with the Lifetime Achievement Award at the Hollywood Makeup Artist and Hair Stylist Awards in 2001, Bob Schiffer was one of the Hollywood greats who was never seen in a film—but without his off-screen artistry, Disney's on-screen magic wouldn't have sparkled half as brightly.

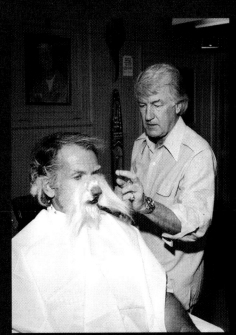

ABOVE: Makeup master Bob Schiffer transforms Dean Jones into a furry sheepdog for the Disney comedy *The Shaggy D.A.* (1976).

DISNEY'S DISTRIBUTION DIRECTOR

"Don't underestimate the public," Irving Ludwig once said. "They are so smart." There could scarcely have been a more perfect fit with Walt Disney's philosophy about his movie audiences than Irving, past president of Buena Vista Distribution, and one of the most respected and innovative executives in the field of motion picture distribution. During his forty-year association with Disney and its distribution arm, Buena Vista, he was an integral force in shaping the structure, policies, and operations for all aspects of releasing Disney movies into the marketplace. Irving passed away at his home in Santa Monica, California, on Saturday, November 26, 2005. He was ninety-five years old.

Born in Lutck, Russia, on November 3, 1910, Ludwig immigrated to the United States with his family in 1920. He was raised in Brooklyn, and went on to study advertising and marketing at New York University. He entered the entertainment industry in 1929 as a part-time usher at New York's Rivoli Theatre, where he quickly advanced to house manager. He held that position until 1938, under both the Paramount-Publix and United Artists theatre circuits.

In 1940, Ludwig opened and operated the Greenwich Village Art Theatre, an independent exhibitor that was the first new movie house in the United States created for the express purpose of screening foreign films. Later that same year, he joined Walt Disney Productions to manage the roadshow engagements of the landmark animated film *Fantasia*.

Ludwig recalled, "It was hard to get theaters to play *Fantasia* because most were controlled by chains. We wanted the film to be an event, and we even purchased old legitimate theaters to present it in. Several didn't even have projection booths. It was quite a challenge."

In 1945, he became a member of the sales administrative staff of Walt Disney Productions. When Buena Vista Distribution Company was formed in 1953, Ludwig was an integral force on the formulating committee that gave the company its structure and launched it into active operation. He became president of Buena Vista in 1959 and held that post until his retirement in October 1980.

He successfully guided the release of such Disney blockbusters as *The Shaggy Dog*, *One Hundred and One Dalmatians*, *The Parent Trap*, *The Absent-Minded Professor*, *The Jungle Book*, and *The Love Bug*, among others. With the 1964 launch of Walt Disney's masterpiece, *Mary Poppins*, Ludwig had one of his most satisfying box office triumphs. He recalled, "We realized that we had a wonderful, magical film and knew the audiences would love it." Under his leadership, reissues of classic Disney animated features also found new success and added to the Studio's reputation for quality family entertainment.

Commenting on Ludwig's passing, Dick Cook, chairman of The Walt Disney Studios, said, "Irving was a keen businessman, a great showman, and a major force in shaping our industry. He was also a great friend and mentor, and he helped to train many of today's top executives. I am deeply indebted to him and will miss his wisdom and guidance very much."

Roy E. Disney, director emeritus and consultant for The Walt Disney Company, added, "He was a caring and dynamic man who was passionately devoted to the Studio and quality family entertainment. His work here at Disney is legendary and he continues to inspire us today."

BELOW: Irving Ludwig in his office at the Walt Disney Studios in Burbank.

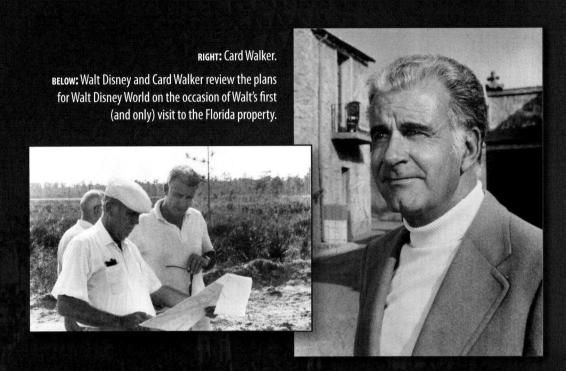

FROM MAIL ROOM TO BOARD ROOM

E. Cardon "Card" Walker was proof of the often-cited (but rarely seen) movie studio executive who rose from an entry-level position in the mailroom to head up the entire company. Card passed away at his La Canada home on Monday, November 29, 2005, at the age of 89.

Card Walker was born January 9, 1916, in Rexburg, Idaho, and moved to Southern California in 1924. He joined The Walt Disney Studio in 1938 (yes, delivering mail), moved on to work in the camera and story departments, then as unit manager on short subjects, after which he moved into advertising and sales, rising to become the company's vice president of marketing. In 1960, he was elected to Disney's board of directors and served on its three-man executive committee.

Card worked closely with Walt and Roy O. Disney on many memorable projects, among them the New York World's Fair attractions "it's a small world" and Great Moments with Mr. Lincoln, Disneyland attractions such as Pirates of the Caribbean and The Haunted Mansion, and blockbuster film releases, including *One Hundred and One Dalmatians*, *The Jungle Book*, and *Mary Poppins*. He was a key participant in the purchase and development of the 27,000 acres in Central Florida that became Walt Disney World.

Card became executive vice president and chief operating officer following the death of Walt Disney in 1966, and led The Walt Disney Company for nearly a decade and a half following the death of co-founder Roy O. Disney in 1971.

That year, Card was named president of the company, and in 1976, he added the duties of chief executive officer. In 1980, he was elected chairman of the board, and under his leadership, the company expanded with such major projects as the development of Epcot at Walt Disney World, Tokyo Disneyland, and the creation of The Disney Channel in the then-nascent cable industry. He retired as CEO and chairman in 1983, but continued to serve as a consultant until 1990.

"I was deeply saddened to learn of the passing of Card Walker," said Robert Iger, president and CEO of The Walt Disney Company. "Card was instrumental in keeping Disney strong and growing in the critical years that followed the passing of founders Walt and Roy Disney. There is little question that, were it not for Card Walker's vision and leadership, Disney would not be what it is today."

"I was privileged to consult with him throughout much of my tenure at the company," said Michael D. Eisner, former CEO of The Walt Disney Company. "Thanks to his deep understanding of the company and its founders, talking to Card was the next best thing to talking to Walt himself."

Disney Insider YEARBOOK
The Contributors

REBECCA CLINE is the assistant archivist in the Walt Disney Archives. She has been with The Walt Disney Company since 1989, and a member of the Archives staff since 1993. She has written articles on Disney history for *Disney Magazine*, the Academy of Motion Pictures Arts & Sciences, and the historical journal, *Persistence of Vision*.

ANTHONY DRAG amassed seven years of experience working in new media and special projects development at The Walt Disney Company before establishing his own business as a freelance writer and multimedia producer. A Georgia native, Anthony received an MFA in Cinema-Television Production from the University of Southern California, and a BA with honors in Philosophy and Comparative Religion from Georgia State University. He currently lives with his wife and cats somewhere in the greater Los Angeles area.

JIM FANNING is a writer, historian, and Disney authority. He is the author of several books, including *The Disney Sing-Along Songbook* and a biography of Walt Disney. His articles have appeared in *The Hollywood Reporter, Disney Magazine, Disney News,* and *Comics Buyers Guide*. Mr. Fanning has written liner notes, behind-the-scenes

books and DVD bonus material for Walt Disney Home Entertainment, and is co-editor and staff writer for *Sketches*, the official magazine of the Walt Disney Collectors Society.

DAVID FISHER began his career with The Walt Disney Company in the Custodial Department at Disneyland more than twenty-five years ago. Now a senior show writer at Walt Disney Imagineering, he writes concepts, scripts, spiels, and nomenclature for Disney parks around the

world. His articles on Disney, its artists, and its history have appeared in *Disney Magazine* and, before that, *Disney News*. He has also written for Walt Disney Records and Buena Vista Home Entertainment.

BRUCE GORDON is a twenty-five-year veteran of Walt Disney Imagineering, where he was a vital force in the creation of dozens of the most popular and beloved Disney theme park attrac-

tions around the world, and is widely regarded as one of the foremost experts on the history and legacy of Disney parks and attractions. A respected author and designer, Mr. Gordon has been the engine behind several important books chronicling the careers of such noted Disney Legends as Academy Award–winning songwriters Richard M. and Robert B. Sherman, and famed artists Herbert Ryman and Peter Ellenshaw.

LESLIE IWERKS is an award-winning film director, producer, and author based in Santa Monica, California. Her diverse documentary and television projects have aired on Bravo, National Geographic, Disney

Channel, and IFC, been released on home video and DVD, and have screened at numerous film festivals around the world.

JEFF KURTTI is the author of more than a dozen books and scores of magazine articles, a writer-director of award-winning documentaries, and a respected public speaker, host, and panel moderator. He is the Creative Director of The Walt Disney Family Library (a project of The Walt Disney Family Foundation), and is considered one of the leading authorities on The Walt Disney Company and its history.

MICHAEL LASSELL is a widely published, award-winning author of poetry, fiction, and nonfiction, whose work has appeared in scores of newspapers, magazines, literary journals, and anthologies. A former theater critic, he holds degrees from Colgate University, the California

Institute of the Arts, and the Yale School of Drama. He lives in New York City, where he is the articles director of *Metropolitan Home* magazine. Previously, he wrote *Aida, Celebration—The Story of a Town*, and complied *Disney on Broadway* for Disney Editions. His next book, *Tarzan—The Staging of a Broadway Spectacular*, is due in stores November 2006.

LEONARD MALTIN, one of the country's most recognized and respected film critics and historians, is now in his twenty-third season with television's *Entertainment Tonight*. He is the author of several books, including *Of Mice and Magic: A History of American Animated Cartoons; The Disney Films;* and *Selected*

Short Subjects. His articles have appeared in *The New York Times, Los Angeles Times, The London Times, Satellite Direct, Smithsonian, Premiere, TV Guide, Esquire, The Village Voice,* and *American Film*. Mr. Maltin teaches in the School of Cinema & Television at the University of Southern California.

TIM O'DAY is a prolific writer and marketing executive who has been associated with The Walt Disney Company for nearly thirty years. As a recognized expert on the subject of Disney, he has worked closely with many famed Disney animators, Imagineers, executives, and celebrities; and

is the author, producer, and host on numerous books, articles, videos, and seminars exploring various aspects of Disney's renowned entertainment legacy.

MONIQUE PETERSON is a writer and contributing editor on numerous books about Disney, art, film, and history, including *The Encyclopedia of Walt Disney's Animated Characters, The Little Big Book of Disney, The Little Big Book of Disney Family Classics,* and *The Little Big Book of Pooh*. She

adapted the Walt Disney Classic Editions storybooks featuring vintage art from the Disney Publishing archives, and co-authored *Mickey Mouse: the Evolution, the Legend, the Phenomenon!* and *Chicken Little: From Henhouse to Hollywood*.

BRIAN SIBLEY is the author of *C. S. Lewis Through the Shadowlands; The Land of Narnia;* and *The Treasury of Narnia*. He also scripted the BBC radio dramatizations of the *Chronicles of Narnia* and edited *The Wisdom of C. S. Lewis*.

PAULA SIGMAN LOWERY enjoyed a twenty-year-career with The Walt Disney Company as an

archivist and writer, and is now pleased to be working for Walt once more as a story lead and archive consultant for The Walt Disney Family Library.

JASON SURRELL is a show writer for Walt Disney Imagineering, and the author of *Pirates of the Caribbean: From the Magic Kingdom to the Movies; Screenplay by Disney; The Haunted Mansion: From the Magic Kingdom to the Movies; The Art of The Haunted Mansion*, and was a contributing essayist

to *The Imagineering Way* and *The Imagineering Workout*. He is currently writing *The Disney Mountains: Imagineering at Its Peak*.

DAVE SMITH, the ultimate authority on all things Disney, founded The Walt Disney Archives in 1970 and three decades later continues to serve as its director. In 1996, he assembled an unprecedented amount of Disney lore,

facts, and figures into an unparalleled reference work, *Disney A to Z: The Official Encyclopedia*, followed by updates in 1998 and 2006. Dave has appeared on numerous television shows as a Disney expert, answers reader questions in a regular column on the Disney Insider Web site, and has attended every Disneyana Convention to date, as a resource person and occasional guest speaker.

CHARLES SOLOMON is an internationally respected critic and historian of animation. He has written on the subject for *The New York Times, TV Guide, Newsweek, Rol Times, Modern Maturity, Film Comment,* and *The Hollywood Reporter*. His books include *The Prince of Egypt: A New Vision in Animation,*

The Disney That Never Was, and *Enchanted Drawings: The History of Animation*, which was a *New York Times* Notable Book of the Year, and the first film book to be nominated for a National Book Critics' Circle Award.

ED SQUAIR has been a researcher in the Walt Disney Archives Photo Library since 1993, digging out seldom seen photographs for publication and display. He's turned a childhood obsession with Disney's Haunted Mansion Attractions into articles for *Disney Magazine* and *The E-Ticket Magazine*. Since 1998, he's been find-

ing the art and writing the captions for *The Disney Days Calender* from Andrews McMeel. In his spare time, he likes to write about himself in the third person.

Index

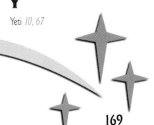

To all who come to this happy place, welcome . . .

50
Happiest Celebration
On Earth

To all who come to this happy place, welcome . . .

Walt Disney

50
Happiest Celebration
On Earth

©Disney

50
Disneyland

Disney's

Insi

YEAR